TEACHER SOURCEBOOK

GRADE 1

PROBLEM-SOLVING EXPERIENCES IN MATHEMATICS

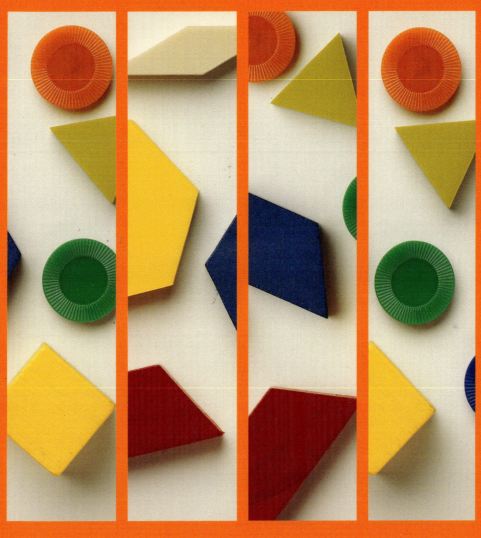

RANDALL I. CHARLES **FRANK K. LESTER, JR.** **ANNE M. BLOOMER**

Dale Seymour Publications®

Problem-Solving Experiences in Mathematics

RANDALL I. CHARLES
FRANK K. LESTER, JR.
ANNE M. BLOOMER

Contributing Writer
MARY B. STURBAUM

TEACHER SOURCEBOOK

GRADE 1

Dale Seymour Publications®
Parsippany, New Jersey

Managing Editor: Cathy Anderson
Project Editor: Mali Apple
Production: Leanne Collins
Design Manager: Jeff Kelly
Text and Cover Design: Christy Butterfield
Illustrations: Cynthia Swann Brodie
Joan Holub
Heather King

Dale Seymour Publications
An imprint of Pearson Learning
299 Jefferson Road, P.O. Box 480
Parsippany, New Jersey 07054-0480

www.pearsonlearning.com
1-800-321-3106

Copyright © 1996, 1985 by Addison-Wesley Publishing Company, Inc.

All rights reserved. Printed in the United States of America. This publication is protected by Copyright and permissions should be obtained from the publisher prior to any prohibited reproduction, storage in a retrieval system, or transmission in any form or by any means, electronic, mechanical, photocopying, recording, or likewise. Blackline Masters excepted. For information regarding permission(s), write to Rights and Permissions Department. This edition is published simultaneously in Canada by Pearson Education Canada.

Dale Seymour Publications® is a registered trademark of Dale Seymour Publications, Inc.

ISBN 0-201-49360-8

5 6 7 8 9 - ML - 06 05 04 03 02 01

This Book Is Printed on Recycled Paper

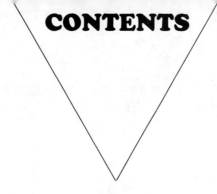

CONTENTS

Overview

Goals of the Program v
Organization of the Program v
Building a Positive Classroom Climate vii
The Teacher's Role viii
Cooperative Learning for Problem Solving xii
Using Manipulatives xiii
Assessing Students xiii
Some Special Considerations xiv

Problem Sets

SET 1	GRANDPA'S TRAIN 1		**SET 11**	CARNIVAL RIDES 65
SET 2	THE HALLOWEEN PARTY 7		**SET 12**	A NEW YEAR'S DAY PARADE 73
SET 3	THE PET STORE 13		**SET 13**	AT THE POND 79
SET 4	COME TO THE FAIR 19		**SET 14**	PIZZA PARTY 85
SET 5	STICKING TOGETHER 25		**SET 15**	PENGUINS IN THE SNOW 91
SET 6	GETTING READY FOR WINTER 33		**SET 16**	HAPPY VALENTINE'S DAY 97
SET 7	THE CIRCUS 39		**SET 17**	MORE VEGETABLES 103
SET 8	A TRIP TO THE ZOO 47		**SET 18**	MORE PETS 111
SET 9	THE CARROT GARDENS 53		**SET 19**	SPORTS AND GAMES 117
SET 10	WINNIE'S TOY STORE 59		**SET 20**	ALL ABOUT DINOSAURS 123

Assessment Appendix 129

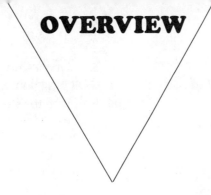

OVERVIEW

"The importance of problem solving to all education cannot be overestimated. To serve this goal effectively, the mathematics curriculum must provide many opportunities for all students to meet the problems that interest and challenge them and that, with appropriate effort, they can solve."
—NCTM Standards, 1989

Problem-Solving Experiences in Mathematics (PSEM) provides the kinds of opportunities described in the NCTM Standards and is designed to supplement any instructional program. It consists of 80 problem-solving experiences grouped by story themes and a teaching strategy for problem solving. A separate package of blackline masters provides students with support material.

PSEM was designed with the NCTM Standards in mind.

Goals of the Program

The ultimate goal of any problem-solving program is to improve students' performance at solving problems correctly. Although this is the ultimate goal, instructional goals need to be more specific and developmental. The goals of PSEM are to

1. Improve students' willingness to try problems and improve their perseverance when solving problems.
2. Improve students' self-concepts with respect to their abilities to solve problems.
3. Make students aware of problem-solving strategies.
4. Make students aware of the value of approaching problems in a systematic manner.
5. Make students aware that many problems can be solved in more than one way, including with the use of manipulatives.
6. Improve students' abilities to select appropriate solution strategies.
7. Improve students' abilities to implement solution strategies accurately.
8. Improve students' abilities to monitor and evaluate their thinking while solving problems.
9. Improve students' abilities to get more correct answers to problems.
10. Improve students' abilities to communicate their thinking.

Organization of the Program

There are four types of problem-solving experiences in this program: problem-solving readiness activities, problem-solving skill activities, one-step problems, and process problems. The 80 experiences in this book are grouped into 20 sets. Each set begins with an introductory story that provides a unifying theme for the experiences in that set.

Problem sets are built around real-world themes.

PSEM provides a problem-solving experience—80 in all—two or three times a week during the school year. The problems were selected and sequenced so the concepts and skills needed to solve each problem would have been introduced to students approximately two months before they are encountered here, *if* the teacher follows the scope and sequence of lessons in most textbooks. For problems at the beginning of the year, concepts and skills are limited to those most students should have encountered prior to first grade. This organization means that students' work is limited to a *review* of concepts and skills. The emphasis on problem-solving instruction can thus be on understanding problems, selecting and implementing appropriate solution strategies, and checking one's work, rather than on carrying out computational skills.

PROBLEM-SOLVING READINESS ACTIVITIES are experiences designed to prepare students for future problem-solving experiences by building their confidence in dealing with real-world situations that involve numbers. Six types of readiness activities are included in Grade 1:

1. Tell how numbers are used in the real world.
2. Given a story, answer questions about information in the story.
3. Tell a story using a given number.
4. Given a story, visualize objects and action in the story.
5. Given a number story, retell the story changing the numbers or the setting.
6. Given a story, act out the action in the story.

PROBLEM-SOLVING SKILL ACTIVITIES are experiences designed to promote the development of thinking processes involved in problem solving. Seven types of skill activities are included in Grade 1:

1. Given a number story, tell a question that can be answered using data in the story.
2. Given a picture, choose/tell a questions whose answer would be found by using addition/subtraction.
3. Given a story problem and the start of a picture, complete the picture to match the story problem.
4. Given the story problem with missing data, choose/tell appropriate data for solving the problem.
5. Given a story problem, tell whether addition or subtraction is needed to find the solution.
6. Given the story problem with missing data, choose/tell appropriate data for solving the problem.
7. Given a story problem, tell whether addition or subtraction is needed to find the solution.

Problem-solving readiness and skill activities build a foundation for problem solving.

PROCESS PROBLEMS are problems that cannot be solved by simply choosing an operation. Instead, process problems are solved using one or more of these strategies:

1. Guess and check
2. Draw a picture
3. Make an organized list
4. Make a table, chart, or graph
5. Look for a pattern
6. Use logical reasoning
7. Use manipulatives

Because process problems cannot be solved by simply choosing an operation, they exemplify and provide practice with the thinking processes inherent in problem solving. The following chart indicates the strategies that can be used to solve the process problems in this book. The chart does not show all of the possible ways of solving the problems—only those that are most commonly used. Also, manipulatives can be used with any of the strategies; their use is incorporated within all of the strategies.

Process problems exemplify and provide practice with the thinking processes inherent in problem solving.

LIKELY STRATEGIES USED IN THE PROCESS PROBLEMS

GUESS AND CHECK
15–16, 39–40, 56, 68, 80

DRAW A PICTURE
11–12, 35–36, 51, 63, 67, 75

MAKE AN ORGANIZED LIST
3–4, 27–28, 55, 67, 79

MAKE A TABLE, CHART, OR GRAPH
19–20, 43–44, 59–60, 71, 76

LOOK FOR A PATTERN
19–20, 23–24, 43–44, 47–48, 59–60, 72, 76

USE LOGICAL REASONING
7–8, 11–12, 31–32, 35–36, 39, 51–52, 64, 75

The two process problems in sets 1 through 12 are matched by probable solution strategies to enable you to teach students how to use problem-solving strategies. Even though the process problems are matched within each of these sets, *it is very important that students are not forced to use the strategy suggested by the hint. In fact, students should be encouraged to find solutions to problems using as many different strategies as they can.*

The process problems in Grade 1 are organized in the following manner.

ORGANIZATION OF THE PROCESS PROBLEMS

SET 1 MAKE/COMPLETE AN ORGANIZED LIST
SET 2 USE LOGICAL REASONING
SET 3 USE A PICTURE
SET 4 GUESS AND CHECK
SET 5 COMPLETE A TABLE
SET 6 LOOK FOR A PATTERN

} The two process problems in each of sets 1–6 are those most students will solve using the strategy shown at the left.

SET 7 COMPLETE AN ORGANIZED LIST
SET 8 USE LOGICAL REASONING
SET 9 USE A PICTURE
SET 10 GUESS AND CHECK
SET 11 COMPLETE A TABLE
SET 12 LOOK FOR A PATTERN

} The two process problems in each of sets 7–12 are still grouped by the most probable solution strategy.

SETS 13–20

} The two process problems in each of sets 13–20 are mixed. That is, students would most likely not use the same solution strategy on each.

Building a Positive Classroom Climate

In the first two months of the school year, the most important goal with regard to problem solving should be to establish a positive classroom climate. Then, you can begin to focus on the development of the students' problem-solving abilities. The importance of a positive classroom climate cannot be overemphasized in building a successful problem-solving program.

In the first two months of the school year, establish a positive classroom climate.

Many factors affect classroom climate. Among the most important are the appropriateness of the content (not too difficult and not too easy), the teacher's evaluation practices, and the teacher's attitude and actions related to problem solving. Of these, the teacher's attitude and actions are most important. Here are some things that will help you establish a positive climate in your classroom for problem solving:

- Be enthusiastic about problem solving.
- Have students bring in problems from their personal experiences.
- Personalize problems whenever possible (e.g., use students' names).
- Recognize and reinforce willingness and perseverance.
- Reward risk takers.
- Encourage students to play hunches.
- Accept unusual solutions.
- Praise students for getting correct solutions, but during problem solving, emphasize the selection and use of problem-solving strategies.
- Emphasize persistence rather than speed.

The Teacher's Role

All of the problem-solving experiences in this book were designed to be given orally, with the teacher playing an active role leading the students through each experience.

USING THE BLACKLINE MASTERS Many of the problem-solving experiences in this book are accompanied by a blackline master (BLM). BLMs provide support material for the problem-solving experiences; *they are not worksheets to be assigned to students.* BLMs can be used only as part of the teacher-oriented, oral problem-solving experiences. A sample BLM for a process problem is shown here. The students should have a copy of each BLM.

USING THE INTRODUCTORY STORIES These stories provide a unifying theme for all of the problem-solving experiences in a set. Each story has an accompanying BLM to be distributed to the students. The stories are to be read by the teacher as the students look at the BLM. The discussion questions given in the teacher notes can be interspersed throughout the reading of the story or can all be asked after the story has been read. The questions do not require mathematics to be answered. Instead, they help familiarize students with the theme, promote the improvement of students' listening skills, and promote the development of students' creativity. The introductory story and discussion questions also serve to motivate students for the problem-solving experiences in the set that follows. If you use a "problem-of-the-day" approach for this program, the introductory story could be read and discussed on Monday and the follow-up problem-solving experiences used on the remaining four days of the week. Some sets may be extended for a longer time.

USING THE LESSON PLAN FOR PROBLEM-SOLVING READINESS AND SKILL ACTIVITIES The lesson plan for readiness and skill activities consists of recommended teaching actions specific to each activity. A sample activity is shown here. The teaching actions provide guidelines for how to (orally) introduce the activity and lead students through a discussion of the activity.

---

17 Readiness Activity

Retell a Number Story

STORY A
Kim saved her allowance this week and bought 4 new stickers. Three were Happy Face stickers and one was a banana sticker.

STORY B
Mindy has more stickers than Joannie. Mindy has 12 stickers and Joannie has 10.

STORY C
Kim's sister really wanted some stickers for her birthday. Kim had 12 stickers but she gave 3 to her sister for her birthday.

TEACHING ACTIONS
1. Read and discuss Story A.
2. Have students retell Story A using different numbers. Solicit a variety of stories.
3. Repeat for Story B.
4. Have students retell Story C using the same numbers but a different context (that is, not about stickers).

USING THE LESSON PLAN FOR PROCESS PROBLEMS AND ONE-STEP PROBLEMS The lesson plan for each process problem and one-step problem is outlined as in the sample shown. Next to each section of the lesson plan are general teaching actions recommended for problem solving. The table on page xi gives a complete description of the teaching actions and describes the purpose of each.

TEACHING ACTIONS BEFORE

1. Read the problem.
2. Ask questions for understanding the problem.
3. Discuss possible solution strategies.

TEACHING ACTIONS DURING

4. Observe students.
5. Give hints as needed for solving the problem.
6. Require students to check back and answer the problem.
7. Give problem extension(s) as needed.

TEACHING ACTIONS AFTER

8. Discuss solution(s).
9. Discuss related problem(s) and extension(s).
10. Discuss special features as needed.

We have found this strategy (i.e., the ten teaching actions) to be a valuable and easily learned plan for facilitating students' thinking and problem-solving work. A scenario is useful to illustrate how to use the teaching actions.

Before students start work on a problem, have a whole-class discussion about the problem, following Teaching Actions 1, 2, and 3. After this discussion, have students begin working on the problem. **During** the time they are working on the problem, move around the room monitoring and directing students' work (Teaching Actions 4, 5, 6, and 7). Near the end of the time students are working on the problem, have two or three students place their solutions on the board. **After** they have solved the problem, have another whole-class discussion about the students' work (Teaching Actions 8, 9, and 10).

One of the key elements in successfully guiding students' problem-solving experiences is asking the right questions at the right time. For each problem, questions and hints are given in the lesson plan. The first set of questions (*Understanding the Problem*) should be used **before** students start work when you are helping them understand the problem (Teaching Action 2). The second set of questions (*Solving the Problem*) should be used **during** the time students are working on a problem, if or when they get stumped in their solution attempt (Teaching Action 5). The hints given for Solving the Problem should be viewed as *possible* hints.

Teaching Actions	Purpose of Teaching Action
BEFORE	
1. Read the problem to the class. Discuss words or phrases students may not understand.	To illustrate the importance of reading problems carefully and to focus on words that have special interpretations in mathematics.
2. Use a whole-class discussion about understanding the problem. Ask questions to help students understand the problem. (See the problem-specific hints for *Understanding the Problem*.)	To focus attention on important data in the problem and to clarify parts of the problem.
3. Ask students which strategies might be helpful for finding a solution. Do not evaluate students' suggestions. You can direct students' attention to the list of strategies on the problem-solving guide when asking for suggestions. (See page xiv.)	To elicit ideas for *possible* ways to solve a problem.
DURING	
4. Observe and question students about their work.	To diagnose students' strengths and weaknesses related to problem solving.
5. Give hints for solving the problem as needed. (See the problem-specific hints for *Solving the Problem*.)	To help students get past blocks in solving a problem.
6. Require students who obtain a solution to check their work and answer the problem.	To require students to look over their work.
7. Give a problem extension to students who complete the original problem much sooner than others. (See the *Problem Extension* section.)	To keep all students involved in a meaningful problem-solving experience until others have completed work on the original problem. (This is a classroom management teaching action. See Teaching Action 9 for using problem extensions to improve problem-solving ability.)
AFTER	
8. Show and discuss students' solutions to the original problem. Have students name the strategies used. You can reinforce the names of the strategies by pointing out the strategy names on the problem-solving guide. (See page xiv.)	To show and name strategies for solving the problem.
9. Relate the problem to previous problems (if possible) and solve an extension of the original problem. (See the *Related Problems* and *Problem Extension* sections.)	To demonstrate that problem-solving strategies are not problem-specific and to help students recognize different kinds of situations in which particular strategies may be useful.
10. Discuss special features of the original problem, if any. (See *Notes*.)	To show how special features of problems (for example, picture accompanying the problem statement) may influence students' thinking.

As you observe and question students, you must decide which, if any, of those hints are appropriate. Sometimes none of the hints listed will seem appropriate, and you will need to come up with others. Quite often you'll find it necessary to repeat one or more of the *Understanding the Problem* questions you used in the whole-class discussion **before** students started work. Most teachers find that selecting just the right hint for a student or group is a teaching skill that develops with experience.

In the *Solution* section, at least one solution to the problem is shown. The names of the solution strategies are given, and the answer to the problem is given in a complete sentence. The solutions shown for each problem were selected because they are ones used most often by students in our work with these problems. However, it is possible that students will use solution strategies different from the ones shown. That's fine! *Students should not be required to use a particular solution strategy for a given problem. Rather, they should be encouraged to find as many ways as possible to solve problems.*

The *Related Problems* section identifies (by number) problems that appeared earlier in the book that can be solved in ways similar to the given problem. The *Problem Extension* section includes an additional problem that is similar to the original problem. The answer to the problem extension is provided after the problem statement. Some problems have a *Comment* section containing an observation about the problems that could be used with Teaching Action 10 (discuss any special features of the problem). For example, some pictures accompanying problem statements can be misleading, and a statement to this effect could appear in this section.

TIME NEEDED TO IMPLEMENT THE PROGRAM This chart shows the amount of time you might expect to spend on the introductory stories and on each type of problem-solving experience if you use the complete set of teaching notes. It is important to realize that the time needed for each experience will be greatest at the beginning of the year. This is particularly true if your students have not had prior experience in a problem-solving program.

Type of experience	*Approximate time required*
introductory story	10 to 15 minutes
readiness and skill activity	5 to 10 minutes
process problem	15 to 20 minutes
one-step problem	5 to 10 minutes

One of the key elements in successfully guiding students' problem-solving experiences is asking the right questions at the right time.

Cooperative Learning for Problem Solving

The introductory stories should be handled as a whole-class discussion. We recommend that students work individually on readiness activities, skill activities, and one-step problems. For process problems, we recommend small-group work. Since process problems are usually challenging, small-group work helps reduce the pressure on the individual student, and it provides a structure for more easily monitoring and assessing the problem-solving performance of all the students in the class. Third, small-group work often elicits behaviors, such as justifying and evaluating ideas, that promote the improvement of problem-solving performance.

One of the important aspects in building successful cooperative group work for problem solving is to establish a class set of guidelines for working in groups. Consider devoting one class session at the start of the school year to developing a class set of guidelines. Invite students, working in groups, to list what they believe should be appropriate guidelines. Then, as a whole class, agree on a final list. Make a bulletin board displaying the guidelines, and refer to them on a regular basis before and after group work. Try not to have too many rules. Here are some guidelines students have suggested.

POSSIBLE SMALL-GROUP RULES
- Include everybody in the group.
- Share ideas.
- Talk only to your group.
- Participate.
- Cooperate with others.
- Pay attention.
- Be polite and kind to others.
- Listen.
- Follow directions.
- Talk quietly.
- Disagree when appropriate.
- Ask group questions only.

Using Manipulatives

Building and using models for important mathematical ideas helps most people to understand mathematics better. Models in the early grades are primarily *manipulative materials*. Manipulatives play a key role in every experience in this program at the kindergarten level and in many experiences at grades 1 and 2.

Suggested materials and tips for their use are provided in the lesson plans. The following manipulatives and other materials are called for in this book:

color counters
tiles
interlocking cubes
blocks
play pennies (*optional*)
play nickels
construction-paper squares and triangles
masking tape
crayons or markers

In many cases, alternative manipulatives can be used. For example, round 1" counters are commercially available, but other materials—such as 1" construction-paper squares, square tiles, buttons, or any other small counting objects—can be substituted for counters, depending on the activity. Alternatives for square 1" color tiles include 1" construction-paper squares and pattern block squares. The key to selecting a manipulative is its intended function in the problem.

Using manipulatives to solve problems may need to be modeled by you or other students to help all understand how the objects can be used to model mathematical situations.

Assessing Students

We have found three types of assessment tools particularly helpful in an assessment plan for problem solving: observations of student work, analyses of written work, and problem-solving portfolios.

An assessment plan for this program should not be limited to a check for correct answers.

OBSERVING AND LISTENING TO STUDENTS Every assessment plan for problem solving must be built on the observations you make as you watch and listen to students as they work. PSEM provides three kinds of support in this area. First, every process problem provides *Strategy Assessment Ideas*, actions and statements related to the implementation of problem-solving strategies to watch and listen for as students solve problems. Second, a *Strategy Implementation Checklist* is provided in the Assessment Appendix (see page 129). This list can be used to record students' progress over time in their ability to appropriately use strategies. Third, a general *Problem-Solving Observation Checklist*, also in the Assessment Appendix, includes general problem-solving behaviors and dispositions to be observed and analyzed over time.

ANALYZING WRITTEN WORK An alternative to observing and listening to students as they solve problems is to use a holistic system for assessing written work, including students' written solutions to problems and, possibly, their written explanations of their problem-solving processes. The Assessment Appendix includes a five-level *Focused Holistic Assessment Rubric*.

USING PORTFOLIOS A portfolio is a collection of student work. Portfolios can be used for many purposes, with the intended purpose determining the contents. A common use of portfolios is to provide a collection of student work that can be analyzed for growth over time. The work may be chosen by the student, by the teacher, or by both. Some possible kinds of work to include in portfolios are solutions to open-ended problems, a report of a group project, a mathematical autobiography, teacher-completed checklists, notes from an interview or observation, and a letter from the student to the reader of the portfolio. The Assessment Appendix includes a *Mathematics Portfolio Profile Checklist* for analyzing a student's portfolio for growth over time.

Here are some important things to keep in mind as you build your assessment plan for problem solving.

1. Assessment is not synonymous with grading.
2. An assessment plan should provide data useful in making instructional decisions.
3. All assessment plans should include observations and questioning of students.
4. Assessment should not be based on a single experience, but should look at student growth over time in a variety of kinds of experiences.
5. Every student does not have to be assessed in every problem-solving experience.
6. Assess thinking processes as well as the correct answer.
7. Assess attitudes and beliefs as well as performance.
8. Inform your students of your assessment plan.

Some Special Considerations

VALUE OF THE INTRODUCTORY STORIES Since students are not asked to solve mathematics problems in the discussions of the introductory stories, it is possible to underestimate the value of these stories. At the early grades, the context of the story is a problem characteristic that significantly affects students' abilities to understand problems. Although we have found the themes in this book to be interesting and familiar to most children, omitting an introductory story could influence their opportunity for success on the problem-solving experiences in that set.

REORGANIZING THE PROBLEM-SOLVING EXPERIENCES Should you decide to use only some of the problem-solving experiences in this book, the organization of the experiences has implications for how you should select and use them. *Do not start in the middle of the book.* The problem-solving experiences have been sequenced from easy to difficult. Even if you do not start the program near the beginning of the year, you should still begin with the first problem-solving experience in the book and move sequentially through the program.

A PROBLEM-SOLVING GUIDE Many teachers find the problem-solving guide shown below to be a helpful instructional aid in implementing the teaching actions for one-step and process problems. Most teachers make a bulletin board out of the guide, while some reproduce copies of the guide for individual students. The guide is particularly helpful for implementing Teaching Actions 3 and 8. For Teaching Actions 3 and 8, students use the guide when suggesting strategies that might be helpful in solving a given problem (Teaching Action 3) and in naming strategies actually used to solve problems (Teaching Action 8).

PROBLEM-SOLVING STRATEGIES GUIDE

- Guess and Check
- Draw a Picture
- Use Addition
- Use Subtraction
- Make an Organized List
- Make a Table
- Look for a Pattern
- Use Logical Reasoning
- Use Objects

DEVELOP AN ASSESSMENT PLAN THAT IS COMPLETE YET EASY TO USE No one assessment technique can capture all aspects of students' thinking related to problem solving. So, build an assessment plan that looks at student work in several ways (e.g., observations, portfolios, written work), but be careful that your plan is reasonable to implement in the time available. It is better to use two or three assessment techniques well than several techniques poorly.

SET 1

Grandpa's Train

Jenny's grandpa worked on a railroad train. He was the engineer. His job was to drive the train. He always wore a hat and scarf when he drove the train, and he sat in the very first car on the train, called the engine.

The engine had a handle in it that you pulled to make the train go faster and pushed to make the train go slower. When the train came to a city, Jenny's grandpa's job was to slow the train by pushing in the handle and to blow the train whistle to tell everyone to watch out for the train.

The train that Jenny's grandpa worked on was a freight train. It usually carried wood and coal and sometimes animals. Some trains carry people, but Jenny's grandpa never worked on a train like that.

Every time Jenny saw her grandpa, he told her a story about the railroad. Jenny missed her grandpa when he wasn't visiting. She would think of him whenever she heard a train's whistle blow.

Discussion Questions

1. What was Jenny's grandpa's job on the train? (*engineer*)
2. When a train came to a city, what did her grandpa do? (*slow down the train and blow the whistle*)
3. What do railroad trains ride on? (*tracks*)
4. Why do trains blow their whistles? (*to tell people to watch out for the train*)
5. Why do people ride on trains?

1 ▸ READINESS ACTIVITY

Tell How Numbers Are Used in the Real World

Story

A train comes through Jenny's town two times each day. When a train crosses a road, all the cars have to stop and wait for the train to pass. Sometimes the cars have to wait a long time before they can drive across the train tracks.

Questions

1. What number is on the train engine? (*3*) Do all train engines have the same number? (*no*) Why do you think numbers are put on train engines? (*to identify the engines*)

2. How many cars are waiting for the train to pass? (*at least 1*) Can you find the car's license plate? Why do cars have numbers on their license plates? (*to identify the cars*)

3. Can you find a picture of an animal? The sign tells us when Dawson Zoo opens. What does the 15 tell you? (*the date in April that the zoo opens*)

4. Can you find a mailbox? The number on the mailbox is 209. Do you have a number on your mailbox (*or house*)? Why do mailboxes (*houses*) have numbers? (*to identify the houses*)

TEACHING ACTIONS

1. Read and discuss the story.
2. Using the questions given, discuss how numbers are used in the picture.

2 ▷ READINESS ACTIVITY

Tell a Number Story

Story
Each train engine has a number on it. Train engines are often black, and the number on each engine is usually white. Jenny's grandpa drove a train with the number 3 on it.

Task 1
Tell a story about a train with the number 4 on it.

Task 2
Tell a story about a train with the number 2 on it.

TEACHING ACTIONS

1. Read and discuss the story.
2. Give Task 1 to the students. Encourage students to make up challenging stories. Solicit a variety of stories.
3. Repeat for Task 2.

3 ▸ PROCESS PROBLEM

Jenny's grandpa likes trains so much that he builds toy train cars and paints them different colors. His favorite train cars are the engine and the caboose. He has a red engine and a blue engine in the same box. He has a green caboose and a yellow caboose in another box. Jenny was playing with the engines and cabooses, and she found 4 different ways to put an engine with a caboose. Can you find the 4 ways?

MATERIALS

red, blue, yellow, and green interlocking cubes (3 of each color per group); crayons or markers in the same colors

Understanding the Problem

- What kinds of train cars are Jenny's grandpa's favorites? (*engine and caboose*)
- What are the colors of the engines her grandpa keeps in the same box? (*red and blue*)
- What are the colors of the cabooses he keeps in the same box? (*green and yellow*)
- How many different ways did Jenny find to put an engine with a caboose? (*4*)

Solving the Problem

- If Jenny chooses a red engine, could her caboose be red? (*no, only engines are red*)
- Could her caboose be blue? (*no, only engines are blue*)
- What color cabooses can be used with a red engine? (*green and yellow*) What color cabooses can be used with a blue engine? (*green and yellow*)

Use Manipulatives

- Use cubes to show a red engine. What color could the caboose be? (*green or yellow*) Can you show this with the cubes? Can you show this by coloring your paper?
- Can you find another way to make a train with a red engine?
- How many ways can you make a train with a blue engine? Show each way with the cubes.

Solution

Make an Organized List/Use Manipulatives

red yellow

red green

blue yellow

blue green

Problem Extension

If Jenny's grandpa gave her a third engine, a white one, how many different ways could she put the engines with the cabooses? (*2 more ways or 6 in all*)

STRATEGY ASSESSMENT IDEAS

Listen and watch as students work to see if they

- show one engine-caboose combination
- organize the combinations (for example, first find all combinations with the red engine)
- list all possible combinations
- use manipulatives appropriately

4 ▶ PROCESS PROBLEM

Jenny's grandpa wears a hat and a scarf when he drives the train. He has 2 hats; one is blue and the other is green. He also has 2 scarves; one is red and one is yellow. Jenny likes to try on the hats and scarves. How many ways can she wear a hat and a scarf together?

MATERIALS

red, blue, yellow, and green counters (3 of each color per group); crayons or markers in the same colors

Understanding the Problem
- What does Jenny's grandpa wear when he drives the train? (*a hat and a scarf*)
- How many hats does he have? (*2*) What colors are they? (*blue and green*)
- How many scarves does he have? (*2*) What colors are they? (*red and yellow*)
- What are we trying to find? (*how many ways Jenny can wear a hat and scarf together*)

Solving the Problem
- Pick one hat. What color did you pick? Now pick one scarf. What color did you pick? Try picking a different pair.
- If Jenny wears a blue hat, what color scarf could she wear? (*red or yellow*) What other color scarf could she wear? (*whichever color was not named first*) Can you show these by coloring the hats and scarves?

Use Manipulatives
- What color counters show the hats? (*blue and green*) The scarves? (*red and yellow*)
- Put a blue counter on the hat. Use the counters for the scarves to show one combination. Color that combination on your paper. Now use the green counter for the hat. Use the counters to show what combinations are possible with the green hat. Color those combinations on your paper.

STRATEGY ASSESSMENT IDEAS

Listen and watch as students work to see if they
- show one hat-scarf combination
- organize the combinations (for example, first find all combinations with the blue hat)
- list all possible combinations
- use manipulatives appropriately

Solution
Make an Organized List/Use Manipulatives

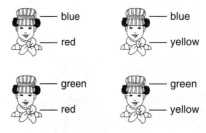

Related Problem: 3

Problem Extension
Suppose Jenny found 2 pairs of boots, black and brown, and 2 pairs of gloves, white and purple. How many different ways could she wear one pair of gloves and one pair of boots? (*4*)

SET 2

The Halloween Party

The children in the first grade class of Ms. Rodriguez were excited. Halloween was coming and the class was going to have a party. Mary said, "I like Halloween because you get to make jack-o'-lanterns." Brett said, "I like Halloween because you get to wear scary costumes and masks." Juanita said, "Yes, and I like Halloween because you go trick-or-treating." Billy said, "Halloween is my favorite day because you get to do all those things."

When the day of the party came, Ms. Rodriguez brought in some pumpkins to carve for jack-o'-lanterns. The children brought costumes and masks from home and wore them during the party. Some of the costumes were scary (but not really), some were pretty, and some were funny. Carrie wore a fairy godmother costume. Kim wore a big bird costume. Joe wore a pig mask.

They also played games. All the children liked bobbing for apples the best. When the party was over, everyone agreed that Halloween really was one of the most exciting days of the year.

Discussion Questions

1. Why were the children in Ms. Rodriguez's class excited? (*Halloween was coming*)
2. Who was Ms. Rodriguez? (*first grade teacher*)
3. What game did the children like the best? (*bobbing for apples*)
4. If you went to a Halloween party, what costume would you like to wear?

5 READINESS ACTIVITY

Answer Questions About a Story

Story A
Ms. Rodriguez brought apples to school on Halloween to play bobbing for apples. She brought 6 red apples and 3 green apples.

Questions for Story A
1. What did Ms. Rodriguez bring to school? (*apples*)
2. How many red apples did she bring? (*6*) How many green apples? (*3*)
3. What game was the class going to play with the apples? (*bobbing for apples*)

Story B
At the Halloween party, the children wore costumes. Four children were dressed in animal costumes. Two children wore ghost costumes, and 3 children wore astronaut outfits.

Questions for Story B
1. Why did the children wear costumes? (*it was Halloween*)
2. How many children wore animal costumes? (*4*)
3. How many children wore ghost costumes? (*2*)
4. How many children were dressed like astronauts? (*3*)
5. Which of those costumes would you like to wear to a Halloween party?

TEACHING ACTIONS

1. Read Story A.
2. Ask the questions for Story A.
3. Repeat for Story B.

6 ▷ READINESS ACTIVITY

Visualize a Story

Note: You may want to discuss the game Pin the Tail on the Donkey with students before reading Story A to them.

Story A
At the Halloween party, the children played a game called Pin the Tail on the Donkey. To play this game, a picture of a donkey without a tail is put on the bulletin board. A child is blindfolded. The teacher gives the child a paper tail with a push pin in it. The child tries to pin the tail on the donkey where it belongs.

Story B
The children at the Halloween party voted on the scariest and funniest costumes. They decided Joe's gorilla costume was the scariest and Jill's clown costume was the funniest.

TEACHING ACTIONS

1. Have students close their eyes.
2. Tell them to picture in their minds the story you will read.
3. Read Story A.
4. Ask students to describe what they visualized.
5. Repeat for Story B.

7 ▶ PROCESS PROBLEM

The children in Ms. Rodriguez's class made 5 jack-o'-lanterns. After they made the jack-o'-lanterns, the class played a game. Here is how the game is played. Ms. Rodriguez put a big red marble in one of the jack-o'-lanterns when the children weren't looking. Then she gave the children 3 clues about which jack-o'-lantern the marble was in. You can play this game too. Look at the picture and use the clues to find where Ms. Rodriguez put the marble.

MATERIALS

counters (5 per group)

Understanding the Problem

- What is a jack-o'-lantern? (*a carved pumpkin*)
- How many jack-o'-lanterns did the children make? (*5*)
- What did Ms. Rodriguez put inside one of the jack-o'-lanterns? (*a big red marble*)
- What is a clue? (*a hint*)

Note: You may want to discuss how to make a jack-o'-lantern.

Solving the Problem

- What is a stem? (*the handle on top of the pumpkin*)
- Which jack-o'-lanterns have smiles? frowns? (*see picture*)
- How many teeth does each jack-o-lantern have? (*see picture*)
- Read clues to the class—slowly, one clue at a time.
- Can you place an X beside a jack-o'-lantern for each clue? (*see picture*)

Use Manipulatives

- Place one counter on each jack-o'-lantern.
- Take off a counter if you know that jack-o'-lantern is not the one being described.
- The first clue tells us about which jack-o'-lanterns? (*the two without stems*)
- Keep taking off counters until there is only one left.

Clues

1. I have a stem.
2. I have a smile.
3. I have 3 teeth.

Who am I?

Solution

Use Logical Reasoning/Use Manipulatives

Clue 1 tells us it is jack-o'-lantern 2, 4, or 5.
Clue 2 tells us it is jack-o'-lantern 4 or 5.
Clue 3 tells us it is jack-o'-lantern 4.

Problem Extensions

1. Give different clues, for example:
   a. I have △ eyes.
   b. I have a frown.
   c. I have 1 tooth. (*1*)

2. Use clues to play the same game with numbers, for example:
   a. I am more than 5.
   b. I am less than 8.
   c. I am less than 7. (*6*)

STRATEGY ASSESSMENT IDEAS

Listen and watch as students work to see if they

- use a plan for eliminating pumpkins that do not satisfy the conditions
- correctly eliminate pumpkins
- arrive at correct conclusions through reasoning

8 ▸ PROCESS PROBLEM

Five boys and girls brought masks to school to wear during the Halloween party. Diana's mask had long ears. Juan wore a mask with a sad face. Kirk's mask had glasses and a funny nose. Beth wore a pig mask. Which mask did Maria wear? Draw a ring around Maria's mask.

MATERIALS

small construction-paper squares or counters (5 per group)

Understanding the Problem

- What did the boys and girls bring to school? (*masks*)
- Whose mask had long ears? (*Diana's*)
- Which mask did Beth wear? (*pig*)
- What are we trying to find? (*which mask Maria wore*)

Solving the Problem

- Help students identify features of each mask. For example, the clown mask has a sad face and the rabbit mask has long ears.
- Can you find the mask Diana wore? Put an X through it. (*rabbit mask*)
- Can you find the mask Juan wore? Put an X through it. (*clown mask*)
- Which mask was Kirk's? Put an X through it. (*mask with glasses*)
- Which mask was Beth's? Put an X through it (*pig mask*)
- Are there any masks that don't have Xs through them?

Use Manipulatives

- Write the children's names on the paper squares, one name to a square.
- As I read the clues, place the paper squares on the masks when you know who the masks belong to.

Solution

Use Logical Reasoning/Use Manipulatives

The gorilla mask is the only one without an X, so Maria wore a gorilla mask.

Note: Encourage students to give reasons why they decided that Maria wore the gorilla mask.

Related Problem: 7

Problem Extension

Suppose Maria, not Diana, had a mask with long ears. Which mask did Diana wear? (*the gorilla mask*)

STRATEGY ASSESSMENT IDEAS

Listen and watch as students work to see if they

- use a plan for recording children's names
- correctly use all conditions given in the problem
- arrive at correct conclusions through reasoning

SET 3

The Pet Store

Mr. Cummings owns a pet store called The Wild Country. The store is very close to a school. Many children love to visit Mr. Cummings' store after school to see the animals. Ralph, Carlos, and Martha stop by every day to say hello to the animals and to Mr. Cummings.

Mr. Cummings' store is not the only pet store in town, but most of the children think his is the best. He has more animals than any of the other stores, and he gets animals from all over the world. One time he had a parrot that said "Hi, there!" whenever the door opened. Mr. Cummings called the parrot Fred. Mr. Cummings has a different name for every one of his animals.

In the back of the store, Mr. Cummings has kittens and puppies for sale. He has kittens of all different colors and puppies of all different colors. Another reason the children like Mr. Cummings' store the best is that he lets them pet the kittens and puppies.

Discussion Questions

1. Where is Mr. Cummings' pet store? (*close to a school*)
2. Is Mr. Cummings' pet store the only pet store in town? (*no*)
3. Do you think Mr. Cummings is a nice man? Why?
4. If you went into Mr. Cummings' store, what animals would you want to see first?

9 ▷ READINESS ACTIVITY

Tell a Number Story

Story

Mr. Cummings has 4 snakes in his pet store. He keeps them in a glass cage at the back of the store. One snake has red marks all over it. Another snake has yellow marks, and 2 snakes are all black.

Task 1

Tell a number story about pets using the number 5.

Task 2

Tell a number story about pets using the number 4.

TEACHING ACTIONS

1. Read and discuss the story.
2. Give Task 1 to the students. Encourage them to make up challenging stores. Solicit a variety of stories.
3. Repeat for Task 2.

10 READINESS ACTIVITY

Answer Questions About a Story

Story A

Mr. Cummings has 2 large cages with kittens in them. One cage has 3 brown kittens. The other cage has 4 kittens of all different colors.

Questions for Story A

1. What does Mr. Cummings have in 2 large cages? (*kittens*)
2. How many kittens are in each cage? (*3 in one cage, 4 in the other*)
3. Do you know the color of any of the kittens? (*no*)

Story B

Mr. Cummings has 3 cages full of puppies. One cage has 2 brown puppies. Another cage has 4 spotted puppies, and the third cage holds 2 black puppies.

Questions for Story B

1. How many cages of puppies does Mr. Cummings have? (*3*)
2. Two of the cages have the same number of puppies. How many are in each of these? (*2*)
3. What are the colors of the puppies? (*brown, spotted, and black*)

TEACHING ACTIONS

1. Read Story A.
2. Ask the questions for Story A.
3. Repeat for Story B.

11 ▶ PROCESS PROBLEM

Ralph, Carlos, and Martha each bought a pet from Mr. Cummings' store. They each got a different kind of animal. The animals were a bird, a dog, and a cat. Ralph bought a dog. Martha has never liked cats. What kind of animal did each person buy? (*Note:* After students have been given Blackline Master 9, have them draw lines connecting the person to the animal.)

Understanding the Problem

- What are the names of the children? (*Ralph, Carlos, Martha*)
- Did they all buy the same kind of animal? (no) What animals were bought? (*bird, dog, and cat*)
- What did Ralph buy? (*a dog*)
- Who doesn't like cats? (*Martha*)
- If Ralph got a dog, could Martha or Carlos get a dog? (*no*)

Solving the Problem

- Can you draw a line connecting Ralph to the animal he bought? (*the dog*)
- If Martha doesn't like cats, what animal did she get? (*bird*) Can you show this?
- If Martha got a bird and Ralph got a dog, what animal did Carlos get? (*a cat*) Can you show this?

Solution

Use a Picture/Use Logical Reasoning

Related Problems: 8, 7

Problem Extensions

1. If Ralph had bought the cat instead of the dog, which animal would Carlos have bought? (*the dog*)
2. If Martha didn't like birds instead of not liking cats, which animal would Carlos have bought? (*the bird*)

STRATEGY ASSESSMENT IDEAS

Listen and watch as students work to see if they

- use a plan, such as drawing lines to record their reasoning
- correctly use all conditions given in the problem
- arrive at correct conclusions through interpreting the picture and through reasoning

12 ▷ PROCESS PROBLEM

There are 3 dogs for sale at Mr. Cummings' pet store. Mr. Cummings named the dogs Sam, Sparty, and Pepper. Pepper is the largest dog. Sparty is smaller than Sam. Which dog is the smallest? (*Note:* After students have been given Blackline Master 10, have them draw lines connecting the name tag to the dog.)

Understanding the Problem

- What are the names of the dogs? (*Sam, Sparty, and Pepper*)
- Are the dogs all the same size? (*no*)
- Which dog is the largest? (*Pepper*)
- Is Sparty bigger or smaller than Sam? (*smaller*)

Solving the Problem

- Can you draw a line connecting Pepper's name tag to the correct dog? How did you know which dog is Pepper? (*he is the largest dog*)
- If Sparty is smaller than Sam, can you tell which dog is Sparty? (*the smallest one*) Can you draw a line to show this?
- If Pepper is the largest dog and Sparty is the smallest dog, which dog is Sam? (*the middle-sized dog*) Can you draw a line to show this?

Solution

Use a Picture/Use Logical Reasoning

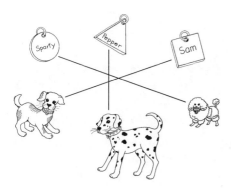

Related Problems: 11, 8, 7

Problem Extensions

1. Suppose Pepper were the smallest dog, not the largest. Then which dog is the largest? (*Sam*)
2. Suppose Pepper were the middle-sized dog, not the largest. Then which dog is the largest? (*Sam*)

STRATEGY ASSESSMENT IDEAS

Listen and watch as students work to see if they

- use a plan, such as drawing lines to record their reasoning
- correctly use all conditions given in the problem
- arrive at correct conclusions through interpreting the picture and through reasoning

SET 4

Come to the Fair

In many places there is a county fair once a year. When the county fair begins, people drive a long way to join in the fun and excitement. For an exciting time at the fair, you can ride on a merry-go-round or a Ferris wheel. You can play games and win prizes like a teddy bear, or you can look at farm animals and all sorts of good vegetables and fruits that people have grown. If you are hungry, you can buy good things to eat and drink like corn on the cob, watermelon, lemonade, and apple cider.

Blue ribbons are given to the people who have raised the healthiest calf, the fattest pig, and the strongest bull. Blue ribbons are also given to the people who have grown the reddest tomato, the sweetest corn, or the biggest pumpkin. Other ribbons are given for the best-tasting cakes and pies, jams, and breads.

A county fair is a kind of celebration. It is a celebration that brings people together to share the good things that nature gives us and to have a good time.

Discussion Questions

1. What kinds of rides are at a county fair? (*merry-go-round, Ferris wheel*)
2. Why do people like to go to fairs? (*fun and excitement*)
3. What would you do first if you went to a fair?
4. What animal would you raise to show at a fair?

13 ▸ READINESS ACTIVITY

Visualize a Story

Story A

At the county fair, Marty and Tony took 2 rides on the merry-go-round. Hal and Beth rode the Ferris wheel 3 times. After they finished their rides, all the children were thirsty, so they bought drinks at the lemonade stand.

Story B

In the afternoon Melissa visited the sheds with the farm animals. She saw 3 very large black pigs. One of them had a blue ribbon on its pen.

TEACHING ACTIONS

1. Have students close their eyes.
2. Tell them to picture in their minds the story you will read.
3. Read Story A.
4. Have students describe what they visualized.
5. Ask them questions about what they visualized.
6. Repeat for Story B.

14 READINESS ACTIVITY

Tell a Number Story

Story

Larry bought a ticket to play a game called Hit the Bottle. To play Hit the Bottle, you get to throw a rubber ball 3 times to try to knock over all the bottles. Larry knocked over 4 bottles in all.

Task 1

Tell a number story about playing Hit the Bottle using the number 5.

Task 2

Tell a number story about playing Hit the Bottle using the number 6.

TEACHING ACTIONS

1. Read and discuss the story and the picture.
2. Give Task 1 to the students. Encourage them to make up interesting stories. Solicit several stories.
3. Repeat for Task 2.

15 PROCESS PROBLEM

Miguel decided to play the Bean Bag Toss. To play this game, Miguel got to toss 2 bean bags into a box. The box is divided into 5 sections. Each section is numbered with one of the numbers 2, 3, 4, 5, or 6. Miguel will win a teddy bear if his tosses make a total of 10. Miguel threw a total of 6. Where did he toss his 2 bean bags? Mark an X on the 2 sections where his bean bags landed.

MATERIALS
counters (12 per group)

Understanding the Problem
- What game did Miguel play? (*Bean Bag Toss*)
- What is a bean bag? (*a cloth bag filled with beans*)
- How many bean bags did he toss? (*2*)
- What would happen if Miguel tosses make a total of 10? (*he'd win a teddy bear*)
- How much did Miguel's 2 tosses total? (*6*)
- Did Miguel win a teddy bear? (*no*)
- What question do we want to answer? (*where did Miguel toss his 2 bean bags*)

Solving the Problem
- What 2 numbers have a sum of 6? (*4 and 2, 3 and 3*)
- Could 2 bags land on the same number? (*yes*)

Use Manipulatives
- How could the number 4 be shown with counters? (*stack 4 counters on the number 4*) How could 2 be shown with counters? (*stack 2 counters on the number 2*)
- Use counters to show what the total would be if his tosses landed in the 5 and the 4.

Solution
Guess and Check/Use Manipulatives
2 + 4 = 6
3 + 3 = 6
6 + 0 = 6
No other sums total 6.

Note: Some students may not notice that 3 + 3 = 6 is a possibility. It is possible to toss both bean bags in the 3 section. Other may not see 6 + 0 = 6 is a possibility, with one bean bag missing the box entirely.

Problem Extensions
1. Change the sum of the 2 tosses to 8. (*5 and 3, 6 and 2, 4 and 4*)
2. Let Miguel have 3 tosses and make the sum 10. (*3, 2, 5*)

STRATEGY ASSESSMENT IDEAS
Listen and watch as students work to see if they
- make guesses that indicate an understanding of the problem
- use previous guesses to make better guesses
- check guesses using the information given in the problem
- give appropriate reasons for their guesses
- use manipulatives appropriately

16 ▶ PROCESS PROBLEM

Tony spent 9 tickets for food when he went to the fair. He saw lots of good things to eat and drink, but he decided to buy 2 things. What 2 things did he buy? Draw rings around what he bought.

MATERIALS

counters (at least 9 per group)

Understanding the Problem

- What did Tony buy at the fair? (*food*)
- How much did Tony spend? (*9 tickets*)
- How many things did Tony buy? (*2*)
- What are you asked to find? (*what 2 things Tony bought*)

Solving the Problem

- What 2 numbers add to 9? (*5 and 4, 6 and 3*)
- Is there more than one way to get a total of 9? (*yes*)
- Could Tony have bought hot cider and a pretzel? (*no*) Why? (*the sum is not equal to 9*)

Use Manipulatives

- Use the counters to show what Tony bought.
- How could 5 tickets be shown with counters? (*stack 5 counters on the popcorn*)
- How could 4 tickets be shown with counters? (*stack 4 counters on the hot cider*)
- On what foods would the counters be placed? (*popcorn and cider, pretzel and lemonade, or pretzel and apple*)

Solution

Guess and Check/Use Manipulatives

6 + 3 = 9
5 + 4 = 9

There are 3 possibilities: pretzel and apple, pretzel and lemonade, and popcorn and hot cider.

Note: Encourage students to find more than one solution.

Related Problem: 15

Problem Extensions

1. Change the sum of the 2 items to 11 tickets. (*hot dog and hot cider or popcorn and pretzel*)
2. Let Tony buy 3 items and make the sum 14 tickets. (*popcorn, pretzel, apple; popcorn, pretzel, lemonade*)

STRATEGY ASSESSMENT IDEAS

Listen and watch as students work to see if they

- make guesses that indicate an understanding of the problem
- use previous guesses to make better guesses
- check guesses using the information given in the problem
- give appropriate reasons for their guesses
- use manipulatives appropriately

Sticking Together

Kim, Mindy, and Joannie started a sticker club. They meet after lunch every Saturday afternoon to trade stickers. Each week they meet at a different girl's home.

The girls keep their stickers in notebooks. Kim has a red notebook, and Joannie and Mindy each have a green notebook. Every Saturday the girls count their stickers to see who has the most. Joannie used to have the most stickers, but now Kim does.

Kim, Joannie, and Mindy have almost every kind of sticker you can think of. All of the girls collect the kind of stickers you can scratch and smell. Kim's favorite scratch-and-smell sticker is grape. Mindy likes the banana stickers best, and Joannie likes strawberry. They all like Happy Face stickers. Joannie likes Happy Face stickers so much she has put one on almost everything she has. When the sticker club ends on Saturday afternoon, the girls look forward to trading new stickers the next week.

Discussion Questions

1. What type of club did the girls start? (*sticker club*)
2. When does the club meet? (*every Saturday afternoon*)
3. Does Mindy have the most stickers of any girl in the club? (*no*)
4. Can you point to the notebook that belongs to Kim? (*yes, it is the one with the most stickers*)
5. If you could buy a scratch-and-smell sticker, what kind would you buy?

17 ▸ READINESS ACTIVITY

Retell a Number Story

Story A
Kim saved her allowance this week and bought 4 new stickers. Three were Happy Face stickers and one was a banana sticker.

Story B
Mindy has more stickers than Joannie. Mindy has 12 stickers and Joannie has 10.

Story C
Kim's sister really wanted some stickers for her birthday. Kim had 12 stickers but she gave 3 to her sister for her birthday.

TEACHING ACTIONS

1. Read and discuss Story A.
2. Have students retell Story A using different numbers. Solicit a variety of stories.
3. Repeat for Story B.
4. Have students retell Story C using the same numbers but a different context (that is, not about stickers).

18 READINESS ACTIVITY

Act Out a Story Situation

Story A

Kim went to Webster's Store to buy some stickers. When she got to the stickers, there was a line of children waiting to buy stickers. There were 4 girls in the line and 5 boys in the line.

Story B

When Kim finally found the stickers she wanted, she and her father got in line to pay for them. There were 3 girls and 4 boys in line in front of them.

TEACHING ACTIONS

1. Read and discuss Story A.
2. Have one student direct others to act out Story A.
3. Repeat with Story B.
4. (optional) For each story, have students count to tell the total number of children in line.

19 ▸ PROCESS PROBLEM

Mindy's favorite sticker is a banana sticker because she loved the smell of bananas. Banana stickers cost 3¢ each. Mindy saved enough money to buy 5 banana stickers. How much money did Mindy have to save for 5 banana stickers? Complete the table to help you answer the problem.

MATERIALS

tiles and counters or pennies (at least 15 of each per pair); crayons or markers

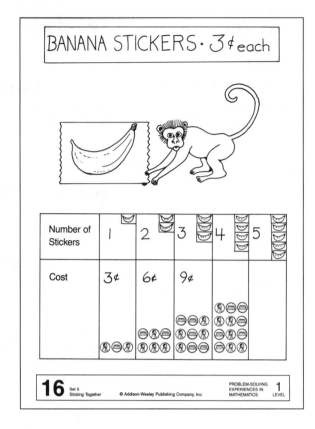

Understanding the Problem

- What kind of sticker is Mindy's favorite? (*banana sticker*)
- How much do banana stickers cost? (*3¢ each*)
- How many banana stickers did Mindy save enough money to buy? (*5*)
- What are the names of the 2 rows of numbers on the table? (*Number of Stickers, Cost*)
- What are you trying to find? (*how much money Mindy had to pay for 5 stickers*)

Solving the Problem

- If one sticker costs 3¢, how much does it cost to buy 2 stickers? (*6¢*) Look at the table. Point to the part of the table that shows that 2 stickers cost 6¢. Count the pennies. Are there 6? (*yes*)
- How much do 3 stickers cost? (*9¢*) Point to the part of the table that tells how much 3 stickers cost. Are there 9 pennies there? (*yes*)
- How much do 4 stickers cost? (*12¢*) Can you count the pennies to find out?
- Can you count on 3 more pennies to tell the cost for 5 stickers?
- Can you draw pennies to find the cost of 5 stickers?

Use Manipulatives

- Use tiles to show the stickers. How many tiles would you put in the first box? (*1*)
- Use counters or play money to show the pennies. How many pennies would you place in the first box? (*3*)
- Using tiles and play money, show the money you need for 2 stickers. How did you decide how many pennies are needed? (*2 groups of 3 pennies are needed*)
  - Use the tiles and play money to help you look for a pattern to finish the table.

STRATEGY ASSESSMENT IDEAS

Listen and watch as students work to see if they

- place items correctly in the table
- use a pattern to correctly extend the table
- interpret the table to arrive at the correct answer
- use manipulatives appropriately

Solution

Complete a Table/Look for a Pattern/Use Manipulatives

Number of Stickers	1	2	3	4	5
Cost	3¢	6¢	9¢	12¢	15¢

Pattern: The cost increases by 3 each time.
Mindy saved 15¢ for the 5 banana stickers.

Problem Extensions

1. How much would 6 banana stickers cost? (*18¢*)
2. If the stickers only cost 2¢ each, how much would it cost to buy 5 stickers? (*10¢*)

20 PROCESS PROBLEM

Joannie's favorite sticker is the yellow Happy Face sticker. She has put a Happy Face sticker on every book she has. Joannie already has 7 Happy Face stickers, but she wants to buy 10 more. You can buy 2 Happy Face stickers for 5¢. How much will Joannie have to pay to buy 10 Happy Face stickers? Complete the table to help you answer the problem.

MATERIALS

counters (30 per pair); nickels (15 per pair)

Understanding the Problem

- What kind of sticker is Joannie's favorite? (*Happy Face sticker*)
- How much does it cost to buy Happy Face stickers? (*2 for 5¢*)
- How many stickers does Joannie want to buy? (*10*)
- What are the names for the 2 rows of numbers in the table? (*Number of Stickers, Cost*)
- What are you trying to find? (*how much Joannie has to pay for 10 stickers*)

Solving the Problem

- If 2 stickers cost 5¢, how much do 4 stickers cost? (*10¢*) Can you point in the table to show this? Count the nickels. Is there 10¢ shown? (*yes*)
- How much do 6 stickers cost? (*15¢*) Can you show this in the table? Count the nickels. Is there 15¢ shown? (*yes*)
- How much do 8 stickers cost? (*20¢*) Can you draw nickels in the table to find the cost?
- Can you draw nickels in the table and count to find the cost for 10 Happy Face stickers?

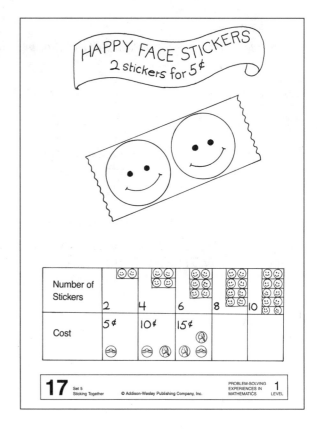

Use Manipulatives

- Use the counters to show the number of stickers in the table and the play money to show the number of nickels.
- How many counters would you put in the first box? (*2*) How many nickels would you put in the first box? (*1*)
- If you want 4 stickers, how many nickels do you need? (*2*) Show that using the money and the counters.
  - Use the counters and the nickels to show the money you need for 6 stickers, 8 stickers, and 10 stickers.

STRATEGY ASSESSMENT IDEAS

Listen and watch as students work to see if they

- place items correctly in the table
- use a pattern to correctly extend the table
- interpret the table to arrive at the correct answer
- use manipulatives appropriately

Solution

Complete a Table/Look for a Pattern/Use Manipulatives

Number of Stickers	2	4	6	8	10
Cost	5¢	10¢	15¢	20¢	25¢

Pattern: The cost increases by 5¢ each time.

Joannie will have to pay 25¢ for 10 Happy Face stickers.

Related Problem: 19

Problem Extensions

1. Suppose you can buy 2 strawberry stickers for 5¢. How much does it cost to buy 10 strawberry stickers? *(25¢)*
2. What would it cost to buy 12 Happy Face stickers? *(30¢)*

Notes

1. Allow students to use play money to solve the problem (and the extension) if necessary.
2. Extension 1 has the same numbers as the original problem. Only the kind of sticker has been changed. This change may lead some students to believe the solution is not the same, but it is.

SET 6

Getting Ready for Winter

If you live where it snows during the winter, there are lots of ways to have fun—sledding, ice skating, skiing, and building snowpeople. When you are through playing, it feels especially good to come into a cozy warm house, sit in front of a fire, and have a bowl of hot soup.

If you were an animal, of course, you would have to find different ways to keep warm and to get food. Many animals that live where the winter is very cold grow heavy coats of fur. Squirrels and other animals that eat nuts and acorns can't find them in winters. They start to save nuts like acorns during the fall before it gets too cold and the snow covers the ground. Squirrels save nuts in special hiding places in trees where other animals can't find them.

What if you were a bird that liked to eat worms? Birds can't save worms. So, when it starts to get cold, many birds fly to warmer places. In warmer places there are more worms to eat. Some birds fly alone, and some fly in flocks. Maybe you have seen a flock of birds fly over your house.

Discussion Questions

1. Why do squirrels save nuts when winter comes? (*so they have food to eat in winter*)
2. What would happen if a bird that lived in a cold place didn't fly to a warm place?
3. What is winter like where you live?
4. Do you know any other animals who have special ways to get ready for winter?

21 ▶ READINESS ACTIVITY

Retell a Number Story

Story

A duck flew south for the winter with 3 other ducks. On the way south they met 4 more ducks who were going to the same warm place.

Task 1

Retell the story with a different number of ducks.

Task 2

Retell the story with bluebirds instead of ducks.

TEACHING ACTIONS

1. Read and discuss the story.
2. Give Task 1 to the students. Solicit stories with different numbers of ducks in them.
3. Repeat for Task 2.

22 ▶ READINESS ACTIVITY

Act Out a Story Situation

Story A
A very large robin flew south for the winter. The robins flew in a line. Two robins flew in front of this large robin. One flew behind her.

Story B
Two squirrels were busy gathering nuts. The squirrels scampered along the ground. They searched under leaves and bushes. When one of them found a nut, it would put the nut in its mouth and hurry back to the tree where the squirrels had built a nest. Later, three more squirrels came by. They each found a nut and put it in the same tree as the other squirrels had put theirs in.

TEACHING ACTIONS

1. Read and discuss Story A.
2. Have one student direct others to act out Story A.
3. Discuss what students have acted out. Ask if it was the same as the story.
4. Repeat with Story B.
5. (*optional*) Have children count to find the number of squirrels in Story B.

23 ▶ PROCESS PROBLEM

Tahir wanted to help the squirrels gather nuts for winter. In his yard, he found acorns of different sizes and colors—some were large and some were small; some were brown and some were yellow. Tahir put the acorns he had found under a tree so the squirrels could find them. He lined up the acorns in a row to make a pattern. Can you decide which acorn Tahir put down next? Color the acorn that comes next in the pattern. (Have students color the acorns brown, brown, yellow, yellow, brown, brown.)

MATERIALS

counters or interlocking cubes (at least 6 in each of 2 colors, such as brown and yellow, per group); crayons or markers in the same colors

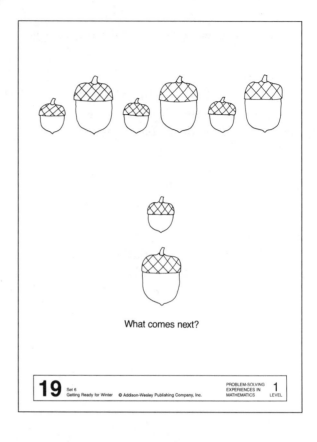

What comes next?

Understanding the Problem
- What did Tahir find? (*acorns*)
- What colors were the acorns? (*brown and yellow*)
- What are we trying to find? (*which acorn comes next*)

Solving the Problem
- How is this acorn (point to second acorn) different from this one (point to the first acorn)? (*large, not small*)
- Repeat the first question for acorns 3 and 2 (*2 large and brown; 3 small and yellow*) and 4 and 3 (*4 large, 3 small*).
- Have students color the acorns as described in the problem statement. What color will the next acorn be? (*yellow*)
- What size will the next acorn be? (*small*)

Use Manipulatives
- Use the counters to show the acorns. What color counters should be placed on the first 2 acorns? (*brown*) On second 2? (*yellow*) On the next 2? (*brown*)
- What color will the next acorn be? (*yellow*) How could it be shown? (*draw an acorn, color it yellow, then place a yellow counter on top of the acorn*) What size will it be? (*small*)

STRATEGY ASSESSMENT IDEAS

Listen and watch as students work to see if they
- describe the pattern
- extend the pattern correctly
- use the pattern to arrive at the answer

Solution

Look for a Pattern/Use Manipulatives

Note: Students should use brown and yellow counters to show the pattern. If they are available, use small counters to show small acorns and large counters to show big acorns.

Pattern: small brown, large brown, small yellow, large yellow

The next acorn is yellow and small. (color the small acorn yellow)

Related Problems: 20, 19

Problem Extensions

1. Suppose the size pattern remained the same, but the colors were brown, then yellow, then brown, then yellow, and so on. Now what kind of acorn will be next? (*small and brown*)

2. Use different patterns; for example

□ △ ○ □ △ ○ □ __

or

▫ △ □ △ ▫ △ □ __

24 ▶ PROCESS PROBLEM

Ruthie Robin flies south when it starts to get cold. One year, as she was preparing for her trip, she went to visit her friends Shirley and Sidney Squirrel to give them her new address so they could write her a letter. But she forgot the number of her mailbox. Ruthie was very sad. "Now I won't get any letters from my friends," she said. Sidney wondered if she knew the numbers of her neighbors' mailboxes. Ruthie did remember those, and she drew a picture of all the nests in her neighborhood and their mailbox numbers. Then Shirley said, "Now we can figure out the number of your mailbox." What is Ruthie's mailbox number? Write the number of her mailbox.

Understanding the Problem

- When does Ruthie fly south? (*when it starts to get cold*)
- Why did Ruthie go to visit Shirley and Sidney? (*to give them her new address*)
- Why was Ruthie sad? (*she wouldn't get any letters from her friends because she forgot her address*)
- What did Ruthie remember? (*the nests and mailbox numbers of her neighbors*)
- What are we trying to find? (*Ruthie's mailbox number*)

Solving the Problem

- What number is on Carl Cardinal's mailbox? (*1*) Daisy Dove's? (*3*) etc.
- Daisy's mailbox number is how much more than Carl's? (*2*) Bert's is how much more than Daisy's? (*2*)
- Let's count by 2s starting at 1: 1, 3, 5, 7, ___.

Solution

Look for a Pattern

Pattern: Each mailbox is 2 more than the one just before it, so 7 + 2 = 9.

The last mailbox number is 9.

Related Problems: 23, 20, 19

Problem Extensions

1. Change the pattern to consecutive even numbers: 2, 4, 6, 8, ___ . (*10*)
2. Put the missing mailbox in the middle of the others, for example: 1, 2, ___ , 4, 5, 6. (*3*)

Note: Some students may not be able to count by 2s starting at 1. (They may say 1, 2, 4, 6, 8, . . .)

STRATEGY ASSESSMENT IDEAS

Listen and watch as students work to see if they

- describe the number pattern correctly
- extend the pattern correctly
- use the pattern to arrive at the answer

The Circus

The Jingling Brothers' Circus is coming to town this weekend! In the Sunday paper, there was a long story telling all about the circus. Anne's father read the story to her, and the more he read, the more excited Anne got about going to the circus.

The newspaper said the circus has 30 elephants! Anne's favorite part of the circus is when the elephants dance in a line. The first time Anne saw the elephants dance, she laughed until her stomach hurt!

Anne's father said his favorite part of the circus is when the lion trainer makes the lions jump through hoops and then into a cage. Anne likes this too, but sometimes she closes her eyes because she's afraid. Anne told her father that sometimes the lions scare her, and her father laughed. Then her father told Anne that the lions sometimes scare him, too! That made them both laugh!

Discussion Questions

1. What is coming to Anne's town this weekend? (*Jingling Brothers' Circus*)
2. What did Anne's father read to her? (*newspaper story about the circus*)
3. How many elephants are in the circus? (*30*)
4. What kinds of acts have you seen at a circus?
5. If you went to a circus, what do you think you would like best? Is there something that might scare you?
6. What kinds of sounds might you hear at a circus?

25 > READINESS ACTIVITY

Answer Questions About a Story

Story A
Five of the elephants know how to dance. Six of the elephants know how to lie down and roll over. Even though the circus lasted 3 hours, Anne wanted to stay and see all of the elephants.

Questions for Story A
1. How long did the circus last? (*3 hours*)
2. How many elephants dance? (*5*)
3. How many elephants lie down and roll over? (*6*)
4. How long did Anne want to stay? (*3 hours*)

Story B
The act where lions jumped through hoops was near the end of the show. The lion trainer's name was Teresa. She had 7 lions in the cage at the same time. She didn't look afraid, but I would have been.

Questions for Story B
1. Were the lions jumping through hoops near the beginning or near the end of the show? (*end*)
2. How many lions were in the cage at the same time? (*7*)
3. What was the lion trainer's name? (*Teresa*)
4. Did Teresa look afraid of the lions? (*no*)

TEACHING ACTIONS

1. Read Story A.
2. Ask the questions for Story A.
3. Repeat for Story B.

26 SKILL ACTIVITY

Complete a Picture to Show a Story

Picture

Story A

All the circus clowns ate lunch together every day. There were 6 chairs on one side of the clowns' table and 5 chairs on the other side of the table.

Story B

One day for lunch the clowns had apples and bananas to eat. There were 3 round bowls full of apples on the table and 4 square bowls of bananas on the table.

TEACHING ACTIONS

1. On the board, draw a rectangle as shown. Have students copy the picture. Tell them this is a table.
2. Read Story A to the students. Have them draw small circles to show chairs.
3. Show different students' pictures on the board.
4. Read Story B to the students. Have them draw circles and squares to show the bowls on the table.
5. Show different students' pictures on the board.
6. (*optional*) Have students tell the total number of bowls on the table.

27 PROCESS PROBLEM

One of the most exciting shows at the Jingling Brothers' Circus is the one where a lion jumps through hoops and then into the cage. The lion first has to jump through either a square or a triangle. Then the lion has to jump through either a circle or a rectangle. How many ways can the lion jump through the hoops and get into the cage?

MATERIALS

masking tape (on the floor, make a square, a triangle, a circle, and a rectangle with masking tape, each shape big enough for a student to stand in; follow Blackline Master 22 for placement of the shapes)

Understanding the Problem

- What 2 hoops must the lion jump through first? (*square or triangle*)
- What 2 hoops must the lion choose from next? (*circle or rectangle*)
- Can the lion jump through the square and the triangle at the same time? (*no*)

Note: You may need to review the names of the geometric shapes with the students.

Solving the Problem

- Which hoop would you like the lion to jump through first, the square or the triangle?
- Then which two hoops does the lion have to choose from?
- If the lion jumped through the square first, which hoop will he jump through next? (*the circle or rectangle*) Write your choice on the paper.

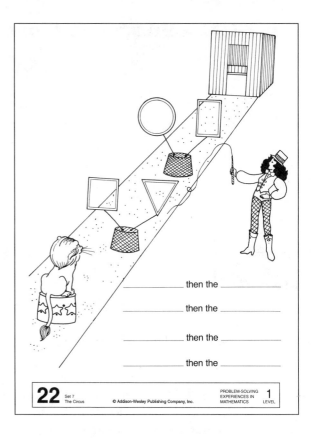

- Have students volunteer to be the lion and to act out the problem by walking through the shapes on the floor. After the first choice has been made, record the answer on the paper. Repeat the process until all 4 ways have been determined.

STRATEGY ASSESSMENT IDEAS

Listen and watch as students work to see if they

- can name one way to jump through the hoops
- organize their lists
- list all possible combinations
- use manipulatives appropriately

Solution

Make an Organized List

□ then the ○   △ then the ○

□ then the ▭   △ then the ▭

Related Problems: 4, 3

Problem Extension

One of the lions will never jump through a hoop that has 4 sides. Which hoops would this lion have to jump through to get to the cage? (*the triangle then the circle*)

28 PROCESS PROBLEM

Elaine is the most famous of the dancing circus elephants. Her trainer always puts her in the same hat, but Elaine wears sneakers and skirts in different colors. She has red sneakers, blue sneakers, and yellow sneakers. She has a green skirt and a purple skirt. There are 6 different sneakers and skirt outfits Elaine can wear. Can you list all 6 outfits?

MATERIALS

red, blue, and yellow counters (5 of each color per group); green and purple counters (5 of each color per group); crayons or markers in the same colors

Understanding the Problem

- How many pairs of sneakers does Elaine wear at a time? *(1)*
- How many pairs of sneakers does Elaine have? *(3)* What colors are they? *(red, blue, yellow)*
- How many skirts does Elaine wear at a time? *(1)*
- How many skirts does Elaine have? *(2)* What colors are they? *(green and purple)*

Solving the Problem

- If Elaine wore red sneakers, name one skirt she could wear with them. *(green or purple)*
- Could she wear the other skirt with them instead? *(yes)*
- How many outfits does this make? *(2)*

Use Manipulatives

- Use the red counters to show the red sneakers and the green and purple counters to show the skirts.
- How could you show the blue sneakers on your paper? *(blue counters)*

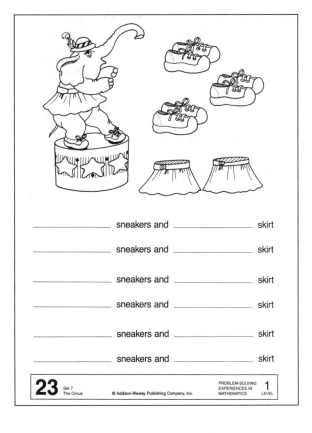

- What color skirt could Elaine wear with them? *(green or purple)* How could you show the green skirt? *(green counter)* the purple skirt? *(purple counter)*
- Using yellow, green, and purple counters, show the other possible outfits.
- Color the shoes and skirts when you are finished.

STRATEGY ASSESSMENT IDEAS

Listen and watch as students work to see if they

- can name one sneakers-skirt combination
- organize their lists
- list all possible combinations
- use manipulatives appropriately

Solution

Make an Organized List/Use Manipulatives

Students should use the counters to show the 6 possible outfits:

red sneakers, purple skirt
red sneakers, green skirt
yellow sneakers, purple skirt
yellow sneakers, green skirt
blue sneakers, purple skirt
blue sneakers, green skirt

Note: Students could mark each blank with the correct color rather than write the color word.

Related Problems: 27, 4, 3

Problem Extensions

1. If Elaine's trainer never put red sneakers with a purple skirt, how many different sneakers and skirt outfits can Elaine wear? *(5)*
2. If Elaine had 2 pairs of sneakers instead of 3, how many different sneakers and skirt outfits could she wear? *(4)*

SET 8

A Trip to the Zoo

Angela and Scott are going to the zoo on Saturday. The zoo is an exciting and interesting place to go because it has all kinds of animals you won't find in pet stores or in your neighborhood—elephants, giraffes, bears, monkeys, lions, and tigers. There are also a lot of different kinds of birds—some with long tail feathers, and some with big, sharp beaks. Some zoos even have kangaroos, hippopotamuses, zebras, and rhinoceroses!

The zoo Scott and Angela will visit has a skyway where people can ride in little cars and look down on all the animals. Angela and Scott want to ride the skyway and watch different animals moving around. They also want to find out what each animal eats.

Discussion Questions

1. Can you name 2 animals you might find at a zoo?
2. Can you point to the giraffe in your picture?
3. What do you think giraffes eat?
4. Which animals would you like to see if you went to a zoo? Why?
5. Why do we have zoos?

29 SKILL ACTIVITY

Complete a Picture to Show a Story

Story

Each morning Ms. Hughes, the zookeeper, puts bananas in the monkey cage for the monkeys to eat when they wake up. There are 5 monkeys, and each monkey eats 2 bananas.

TEACHING ACTIONS

1. Draw 2 bananas on the board (as shown), and have students copy them. Tell students, "There are 2 bananas for one monkey."
2. Read the story to the students. Have them draw bananas for the other monkeys.
3. Show different students' pictures on the board.
4. (*optional*) Ask students to find out how many bananas Ms. Hughes left for the monkeys.

30 READINESS ACTIVITY

Retell a Number Story

Story A
When Angela and Scott were at the zoo, they saw 6 monkeys. Four of the monkeys were eating bananas and 2 of them were eating peanuts.

Story B
Morris and Myrtle Monkey both like to eat bananas. One day Morris ate 11 bananas and Myrtle ate 9. Morris ate more bananas than Myrtle.

TEACHING ACTIONS

1. Read and discuss Story A.
2. Ask students to retell Story A using different numbers. Solicit a variety of stories.
3. Repeat for Story B.
4. Have students retell Story B using the same numbers, but with a different context (that is, not about monkeys eating).

31 ▸ PROCESS PROBLEM

When Angela and Scott were at the zoo, they saw something very interesting—an animal race. The animals in the race were a zebra, a giraffe, a kangaroo, and a lion. The zebra was the fastest. The giraffe was the slowest. The lion finished behind the kangaroo. Who won the race?

MATERIALS

small construction-paper squares or counters (4 per group)

Understanding the Problem

- What interesting thing did Angela and Scott see at the zoo? (*an animal race*)
- Which animals were in the race? (*zebra, giraffe, kangaroo, lion*)
- Which animal was fastest? (*zebra*)
- Which animal was slowest? (*giraffe*)
- Did the lion finish ahead of the kangaroo? (*no, behind*)
- What are we asked to find? (*which animal won the race*)

Solving the Problem

- Which animal won the race? (*the zebra named Zeke*) Write the animal's name in the space above the word WINNER.
- Which animal came in last? (*the giraffe named Clara*) How do you know? Write the animal's name in the last space.
- Where does the lion's name belong? (*after the kangaroo's name*)

Use Manipulatives

- Write each animal's name on a paper square, one name to each paper square.
- On which space will the winner's name be placed? the loser's name?
- Put a paper square in a space as I read the clues. I'll read each clue twice in case you want to change your mind.

Solution

Use Logical Reasoning/Use Manipulatives

Students can use counters for each animal and line them up to solve the problem.

Zeke   Kate   Leo   Clara
Winner

Related Problems: 12, 11, 8, 7

Problem Extensions

1. Who came in second in the race? (*Kate*)
2. Who came in third in the race? (*Leo*)

STRATEGY ASSESSMENT IDEAS

Listen and watch as students work to see if they

- use objects or pictures to keep track of or to record their reasoning
- correctly use all conditions given in the problem
- arrive at correct conclusions through reasoning
- use manipulatives appropriately

32 > PROCESS PROBLEM

Scott and Angela were at the zoo during feeding time for the animals. Zeke Zebra eats hay. Morris Monkey eats fruit, especially bananas. The food Horace Hippo eats the most grows in water. Clara Giraffe uses her long neck to reach her food. What food does Ellie Elephant eat most often? Draw a line from each animal to the food it eats the most.

Understanding the Problem

- What happened when Angela and Scott were at the zoo? (*the animals were fed*)
- What does Zeke eat? (*hay*)
- What is hay? (*dried grass*)
- What is "hippo" a nickname for? (*hippopotamus*)
- What food grows in water? (*grass*)
- Where does Clara's food grow? (*tree*)
- Which animal are we trying to find out about? (*Ellie Elephant*)

Note: A bale of hay may be a new idea. Tell students that zebras eat fresh grass when they are in the wild, but they eat dried grass when they are in zoos.

Solving the Problem

- Can you draw a line from Zeke to what he eats? (*see solution*) Continue for other animals except Ellie.
- Which food does not have a line drawn to it? (*peanuts*)

Solution

Use Logical Reasoning

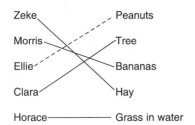

Related Problems: 31, 12, 11, 8, 7

Problem Extension

Suppose Ellie eats 2 types of food—peanuts and something else. She doesn't eat fruit or grass and she can't reach the leaves on the tree. What else can she eat? (*hay*)

STRATEGY ASSESSMENT IDEAS

Listen and watch as students work to see if they

- use objects or pictures to keep track of or to record their reasoning
- correctly use all conditions given in the problem
- arrive at correct conclusions through reasoning

SET 9

The Carrot Gardens

Ricky Rabbit, Mary Rabbit, and Billy Rabbit play together every day in the woods. Ricky is a brown rabbit. Mary and Billy are both white rabbits. Ricky and Mary are the same age. Billy is a lot younger, but that doesn't matter to any of them.

In the summer, Ricky, Mary, and Billy used to eat carrots in Mr. Whipple's garden. Last summer, Mr. Whipple almost caught them, so this spring they planted their own gardens. The 3 rabbits made their gardens different shapes, but they all planted carrots. They planted so many carrots, they thought they may never have to visit Mr. Whipple's garden again!

Billy Rabbit needed Ricky's and Mary's help planting his garden. Every day the rabbits watered their gardens and waited for the carrots to grow. One day, they saw the tops of the carrots. They were all very excited. They knew this was going to be the best summer they had ever had!

Discussion Questions

1. How many rabbits are in this story? (*3*) What are their names? (*Ricky, Mary, Billy*)
2. Are all of the rabbits the same age? (*no*)
3. What did the rabbits plant this spring? (*carrots*)
4. Are the gardens the same shape or different shapes? (*different shapes*)
5. Besides the rabbits, who will be very happy the rabbits planted their own gardens? (*Mr. Whipple*)
6. If you planted a garden, what would you plant?

33 SKILL ACTIVITY

Choose an Addition Question

Story A

Ricky had only 3 carrots left in his rabbit hole. Last night he pulled up 7 more carrots from his garden and put them in his rabbit hole.

Note: The word left in Story A may suggest subtraction to some students. Point out that the word left does not mean subtraction in this story.

Questions for Story A

1. How many carrots did Ricky pull up last night?
*2. What is the total number of carrots Ricky has in his rabbit hole?

Story B

Ricky likes carrots. He eats carrots for breakfast and lunch. Yesterday he ate 3 carrots for breakfast and 5 carrots for lunch.

Questions for Story B

*1. How many carrots did Ricky eat for breakfast and lunch altogether?
2. How many carrots did Ricky eat for lunch?

TEACHING ACTIONS

1. Read Story A.
2. Read the questions for Story A. Have students choose the addition question.
3. Discuss the correct choice.
4. Repeat for Story B.
*5. (*optional*) Have students tell the answer to each addition question.

34 SKILL ACTIVITY

Choose an Addition Question

Picture A
5 carrots on a plate, 2 carrots in Ricky's hand—see Blackline Master 28

Questions for Picture A
1. How many carrots are on the plate?
*2. How many carrots does Ricky have in all?

Picture B
3 eaten carrots on a table, 4 eaten carrots on the floor—see Blackline Master 28

Questions for Picture B
*1. How many carrots did Ricky eat?
2. How many more carrots are on the floor than are on the table?

Note: Both pictures do not show the 2 groups of carrots being put together. Be sure to discuss how the addition questions suggest "put together" even though the pictures do not show this action.

TEACHING ACTIONS
1. Show and discuss Picture A.
2. Read the questions for Picture A. Have students choose the addition question.
3. Discuss the students' choice.
4. Repeat for Picture B.
*5. (optional) Have students tell the answer to each addition question.

35 PROCESS PROBLEM

Billy Rabbit's, Mary Rabbit's, and Ricky Rabbit's carrot gardens are all different shapes. One garden is in the shape of a triangle. Another is a square, and one is a rectangle. Mary's garden is in the shape of a triangle. The sides of Ricky's garden are all the same length. What is the shape of Billy's garden?

Understanding the Problem

- Are the rabbits' gardens the same shape or different? (*different*)
- What are the shapes of the gardens? (*triangle, square, rectangle*)
- Do you know the shape of Mary's garden? (*a triangle*)
- What do we know about Ricky's garden? (*the sides are all the same length*)
- What are you trying to find? (*the shape of Billy's garden*)

Solving the Problem

- If Mary's garden is a triangle, could any of the other rabbits have the triangle garden? (*no*) Can you draw a line connecting Mary to her garden?
- What shape has all 4 sides the same length? (*square*) So, whose garden is in the shape of a square? (*Ricky's*) Can you draw a line connecting Ricky to his garden?
- If Mary's garden is a triangle, and Ricky's garden is a square, what shape is Billy's garden? (*rectangle*)

Solution

Use Logical Reasoning/Draw a Picture

Billy's garden is a rectangle.

Related Problems: 32, 31, 12, 11, 8

Problem Extensions

1. Suppose Mary's garden was the rectangle and Billy's garden had 3 sides. What shape would Ricky's garden be? (*a square*)

2. Suppose Ricky's garden was the triangle and Mary's had 4 sides the same length. Which shape would Billy's garden be? (*a rectangle*)

STRATEGY ASSESSMENT IDEAS

Listen and watch as students work to see if they

- draw lines to match up information in the problem
- correctly use all conditions given in the problem
- arrive at correct conclusions through reasoning

36 PROCESS PROBLEM

Ricky Rabbit, Mary Rabbit, and Billy Rabbit each pulled up one carrot. Ricky pulled up the shortest carrot. Mary's carrot was longer than Billy's carrot. Who had the middle-sized carrot?

Understanding the Problem
- How many carrots did each rabbit pull up? (*1*)
- Were all of the carrots the same length? (*no*)
- Who pulled up the shortest carrot? (*Ricky*)
- Was Mary's carrot longer or shorter than Billy's carrot? (*longer*)
- What are you trying to find? (*who had the middle-sized carrot*)

Solving the Problem
- Can Mary's or Billy's carrot be shorter than Ricky's carrot? (*no, Ricky pulled up the shortest carrot*)
- Can you draw Mary's carrot? Is it longer than Ricky's? (*it should be*)
- Can you draw Billy's carrot? Is it longer than Ricky's? (*it should be*) Is Mary's carrot longer than Billy's? (*it should be*)

Note: Some students may confuse size with length. Encourage students to keep the ends of the carrots aligned.

Solution
Use Logical Reasoning/Draw a Picture

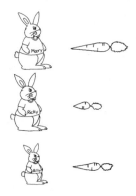

Billy had the middle-sized carrot.

Related Problems: 35, 32, 31, 12, 11

Problem Extension

If Ricky had pulled up the longest carrot instead of the shortest carrot, who would have pulled up the middle-sized carrot? (*Mary*)

STRATEGY ASSESSMENT IDEAS

Listen and watch as students work to see if they
- draw carrots to show information in the problem
- correctly use all conditions given in the problem
- arrive at correct conclusions through reasoning

SET 10

Winnie's Toy Store

It's always fun to go to the toy store, whether you want to buy something or just look. At Winnie's Toy Store you can find toys of all kinds for children of all ages. You can buy big toys and small toys, toys you ride on and toys you kick, hit, or throw. There are toys you play with by yourself and toys you use with others. Any kind of toy you can think of is at Winnie's: bicycles, tricycles, skates; dolls of all kinds and teddy bears of all sizes; baseballs, basketballs, footballs, and soccer balls; toy cars, trucks, airplanes, and spaceships; and board games and computer games. If you went to Winnie's, you would be sure to find your favorite toys.

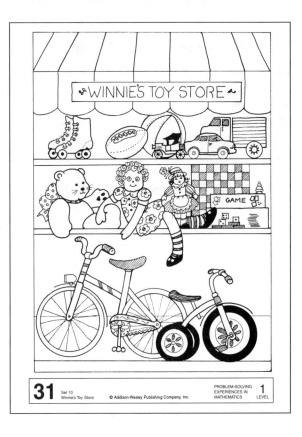

Discussion Questions

1. What is the name of the toy store in this story? (*Winnie's Toy Store*)
2. Does Winnie's have bicycles? (*yes*) Teddy bears? (*yes*)
3. What is your favorite toy? Do you think Winnie's would have it?
4. Do you think Winnie's would have small plastic building blocks that snap together?
5. Have you even been to a toy store? Was it like Winnie's?

37 ▷ SKILL ACTIVITY

Tell an Addition Question for a Story

Story A
There are 4 brown teddy bears and 5 yellow teddy bears on a shelf at Winnie's toy store.

Possible Questions for Story A
How many teddy bears are on the shelf?

Story B
Melinda wants to buy a crayon and a crayon sharpener. Crayon sharpeners cost 6¢ each and crayons costs 4¢ each.

Possible Questions for Story B
What is the total cost to buy a sharpener and a crayon?

TEACHING ACTIONS

1. Read and discuss Story A.
2. Ask students to tell a question that can be answered using addition.
3. Repeat for Story B.

38 ONE-STEP PROBLEM

Laura wanted to buy either a basketball or a football for her birthday. She looked at 5 basketballs and 3 footballs before she decided which to buy. Altogether, how many basketballs and footballs did she look at?

MATERIALS
counters (10 per student)

Understanding the Problem
- Why did Laura look at basketballs and footballs? (*she wanted to buy one for her birthday*)
- How many basketballs did she look at? (*5*) How many footballs? (*3*)
- What are we trying to find? (*the total number looked of basketballs and footballs Laura looked at*)

Solving the Problem
- Are you putting objects together or taking some away in this story? (*putting together*)
- Is this an addition or a subtraction story? (*addition*)
- Can you write or tell a number sentence using the number of basketballs and the number of footballs? (*see solution*)

Use Manipulatives
- Can you use the counters to show the number of basketballs? the number of footballs?
- Put the counters together to find the total number of balls.

Solution
Choose the Operation

$5 + 3 = 8$ or $\begin{array}{r} 5 \\ + 3 \\ \hline 8 \end{array}$

Laura looked at 8 balls in all.

Problem Extension
How many more basketballs did Laura look at than footballs? (*2*)

39 > PROCESS PROBLEM

Lisa looked at some bicycles and tricycles in Winnie's Toy Store. On the bicycles and tricycles she looked at, she counted 7 wheels. How many bicycles and how many tricycles did Lisa look at? Draw a ring around the bicycles and tricycles she looked at.

Understanding the Problem
- What did Lisa look at in Winnie's Toy Store? (*bicycles and tricycles*)
- What did she count? (*wheels*)
- How many wheels did she count? (*7*)
- How many wheels does a bicycle have? (*2*) A tricycle? (*3*)
- Are we only looking for how many bicycles she looked at? (*no, bicycles and tricycles*)

Solving the Problem
- Could Lisa have looked at only one bicycle and one tricycle? (*no, 2 + 3 = 5*)
- How many wheels do one bicycle and one tricycle have in all? (*5*) How many more do we need? (*2*)
- Write down under each group of bicycles and tricycles how many wheels there are.
- What numbers added together make 7? (*see solution*)

Solution

Guess and Check
- Try: one bicycle and one tricycle—5 wheels, need 2 more—add one bicycle to get 7 wheels.
  So, 2 bicycles and 1 tricycle give 7 wheels in all.
- Try: 2 bicycles make 4 wheels—need 3 more—add 1 tricycle to get 7 wheels.
  So, 2 bicycles and 1 tricycle give 7 wheels in all.

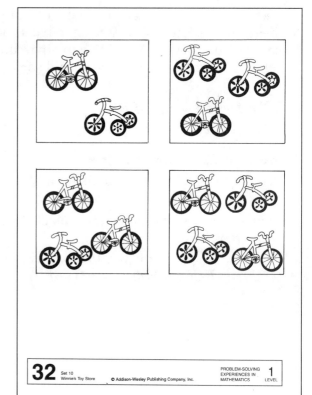

Logical Reasoning

1 bicycle—2 wheels: 7 − 2 = 5 wheels
2 bicycles—4 wheels: 7 − 4 = 3
2 bicycles and 1 tricycle = 7 wheels

Lisa looked at 2 bicycles and 1 tricycle.

Note: Some students may suggest 4 bicycles if they do not use the pictures on Blackline Master 32.

Related Problems: 32, 31, 16, 15, 12

Problem Extension

Suppose Lisa counted 8 wheels? (*2 tricycles and 1 bicycle*)

STRATEGY ASSESSMENT IDEAS

Listen and watch as students work to see if they
- make guesses that indicate an understanding of the problem
- use previous guesses to make better guesses
- check guesses using the information given in the problem
- give appropriate reasons for their guesses

40 > PROCESS PROBLEM

Pete went to Winnie's Toy Store to buy some toy cars and trucks to add to his collection. He spent $9 in all. Which toy cars or trucks did he buy?

MATERIALS

counters or pennies (10 per group)

Understanding the Problem

- What did Pete want to buy at Winnie's? (*toy cars and trucks*)
- What does Pete collect? (*toy cars and trucks*)
- How much money did he spend? (*$9*)
- What do we want to find? (*which cars and trucks Pete bought*)

Solving the Problem

- What numbers add to 9? (*5 and 4*)
- Could Pete have bought a pickup truck and a van? (*no*) Why? (*the sum is not $9*)
- Can you guess which cars and trucks Pete might have bought and then add the costs to check? (*see solution*)

Use Manipulatives

- Stack counters on top of each price. How many counters would you place on $4? (*4*) On $1? (*1*) On $7? (*7*) On $3? (*3*) On $5? (*5*)
- Which of the stacks add up to $9? (*4 and 5*) Put the counters together and count to check.

Solution

Guess and Check/Use Manipulatives

Students should place counters on the numbers and find which stacks add to 9 by counting the counters in the stacks: $5 + $4 = $9.

- Try 7 and 3: 7 + 3 = 10 (*too high*)
- Try 5 and 3: 5 + 3 = 8 (*too low*)
- Try 5 and 4: 5 + 4 = 9 (*correct*)

Pete bought the cars that cost $5 and $4.

Related Problems: 39, 16, 15

Problem Extensions

1. Suppose Pete spent $10 for 2 vehicles. Which vehicles did he buy? (*$7 and $3*)
2. Suppose Pete bought 3 vehicles and paid $12. Which vehicles did he buy? (*$4 + $5 + $3 = $12 or $7 + $1 + $4 = $12*)

STRATEGY ASSESSMENT IDEAS

Listen and watch as students work to see if they

- make guesses that indicate an understanding of the problem
- use previous guesses to make better guesses
- check guesses using the information given in the problem
- give appropriate reasons for their guesses
- use manipulatives appropriately

Carnival Rides

Meela and her brother Kyle asked their mother and father if they could go to the carnival next week. The carnival was going to be set up on their school's playground. The night their mother and father said they could go, Kyle and Meela got so excited that they had trouble falling asleep!

Every day during the week before the carnival, Kyle and Meela would talk about the carnival and plan what they wanted to do. The same carnival came to their school last year, so they knew all the rides that would be there. Kyle's favorite ride was the merry-go-round. Meela's favorite ride was the Ferris wheel, even though she sometimes gets afraid when she is high above the ground.

The carnival was only going to be at the school for one day. It would open at 10 o'clock in the morning and close at 9 o'clock that night. Kyle and Meela sure hoped it wouldn't rain on the day of the carnival!

Discussion Questions

1. Are Kyle and Meela related? (*yes*)
2. What was coming to town? (*carnival*)
3. Why did Kyle and Meela have trouble falling asleep? (*they were excited*)
4. What were their favorite rides? (*merry-go-round, Ferris wheel*)
5. Why did Kyle and Meela hope it wouldn't rain? (*so they could go to the carnival*)
6. What ride would you want to ride first at a carnival?

41 READINESS ACTIVITY

Retell a Story

Story A
Meela always bought a lemonade drink at the carnival. When she got to the lemonade stand, there were 6 other children in the line ahead of her.

Story B
Kyle played a bowling game two times. The first time he played, he scored 8 points. The second time he played, he scored 12 points.

Story C
Meela won 5 toys playing different games. Kyle only won 3 toys. Meela gave Kyle one of her toys.

TEACHING ACTIONS

1. Read and discuss Story A.
2. Have students retell Story A using different numbers. Solicit a variety of stories.
3. Repeat for Story B.
4. Read Story C.
5. Have students retell Story C using the same numbers but a different context (that is, not about toys).

42 ONE-STEP PROBLEM

Kyle and Meela stayed at the carnival all day. For lunch they each had a cheese sandwich, lemonade, and a big juicy apple. It was so hot on the day of the carnival that Kyle drank 6 glasses of lemonade and Meela drank 3 glasses of lemonade. Altogether, how many glasses of lemonade did Kyle and Meela drink?

MATERIALS
counters (10 per student)

Understanding the Problem
- How long did Kyle and Meela stay at the carnival? (*all day*)
- What did they have for lunch? (*cheese sandwich, lemonade, apple*)
- Why did Kyle and Meela drink a lot of lemonade? (*it was a hot day*)
- How many glasses of lemonade did Kyle drink? (*6*) Meela? (*3*)
- What are we trying to find out about Kyle and Meela? (*how many glasses of lemonade they drank altogether*)

Solving the Problem
- Are we taking some glasses of lemonade away in this story or are we trying to find the total? (*find the total*)
- Is the action in this story an addition or a subtraction action? (*addition*)
- If you drank 2 glasses of lemonade and then drank 2 more glasses of lemonade, how many glasses would you have drunk in all? (*4*)
- Can you use counters to show the glasses of lemonade?
- Can you write or tell a number sentence? (*see solution*)

Use Manipulatives
- Use counters to show the number of glasses of lemonade Kyle drank and the number Meela drank.
- Put the groups together and count to find the total.

Solution
Choose the Operation/Use Manipulatives

$6 + 3 = 9$ or $\begin{array}{r} 6 \\ + 3 \\ \hline 9 \end{array}$

Kyle and Meela drank 9 glasses of lemonade.

Related Problem: 38

Problem Extension
How many more glasses of lemonade did Kyle drink than Meela? (*6 – 3 = 3 more*)

43 ▸ PROCESS PROBLEM

Kyle's favorite ride at the carnival is the merry-go-round. His favorite animal on the merry-go-round is the lion with the big saddle on its back. One ride on the merry-go-round takes 2 tickets. Kyle wanted to take 6 rides on the merry-go-round. How many tickets did Kyle need? Complete the table to help you find out.

MATERIALS

counters (65 per group)

Understanding the Problem

- What was Kyle's favorite ride at the carnival? (*the merry-go-round*)
- How many times did Kyle want to ride the merry-go-round? (*6*)
- How many tickets did it take for each ride on the merry-go-round? (*2*)
- What are the names of the 2 rows of numbers in the table? (*Number of Rides; Number of Tickets Needed*)
- What are you trying to find? (*the number of tickets Kyle needed for 6 rides*)

Solving the Problem

- For 2 rides, how many tickets are needed? (*4; see the table*) Are there 4 tickets shown? (*yes*)
- How many tickets are needed for 4 rides? (*8; see the table*)
- For each additional ride, how many more tickets does Kyle need? (*2*)
- Can you find how many tickets are needed for 5 rides? (*see solution*)

Use Manipulatives

- Place 1 counter in the Number of Rides box. Stack 2 counters beneath it to show the number of tickets. Use counters to complete the table up to 3 rides.
- How many more counters do you place in each box? (*2*)
- How many counters should you place in the fifth box? (*10*)
- How many counters should you place in the sixth box? (*12*) How many tickets does Kyle need for 6 rides? (*12*)

STRATEGY ASSESSMENT IDEAS

Listen and watch as students work to see if they

- place items correctly in the table
- use a pattern to correctly extend the table
- interpret the table to arrive at the correct answer
- use manipulatives appropriately

Solution

Complete a Table/Look for a Pattern/Use Manipulatives

Students should use counters on top of the table to show the number of tickets needed.

Number of Rides	1	2	3	4	5	6
Number of Tickets Needed	2	4	6	8	10	12

Pattern: The number of tickets needed increases by 2 each time. Kyle needs 12 tickets for 6 rides.

Related Problems: 24, 23, 20, 19

Problem Extensions

1. How many tickets are needed for 7 rides on the merry-go-round? (*14*)
2. A roller coaster ride takes 2 tickets for one ride. How many tickets would Kyle need if he wanted to take 4 roller coaster rides? (*8*)

44 PROCESS PROBLEM

Meela couldn't wait to ride the Ferris wheel at the carnival. When she got to the Ferris wheel, there was a long line of children waiting to ride it. The Ferris wheel has 5 chairs. Each chair holds 3 children. How many children can ride on the Ferris wheel at one time?

MATERIALS

counters (at least 45 per group)

Understanding the Problem

- Which ride at the carnival did Meela want to ride? (*the Ferris wheel*)
- How many chairs are on the Ferris wheel? (*5*)
- How many children can ride in each chair? (*3*)
- What are the names of the 2 rows of numbers in the table? (*Number of Chairs, Number of Children*)
- What are you trying to find? (*total number of children that can ride the Ferris wheel*)

Solving the Problem

- How many children can sit in 2 chairs? (*6*) Can you point to where the table shows this?
- How many children can sit in 3 chairs? (*9*) Can you point to where the table shows this?
- Can you find how many children can sit in 4 chairs? (*12*)

Use Manipulatives

- Stack counters in the boxes to show the number of children in the chairs.

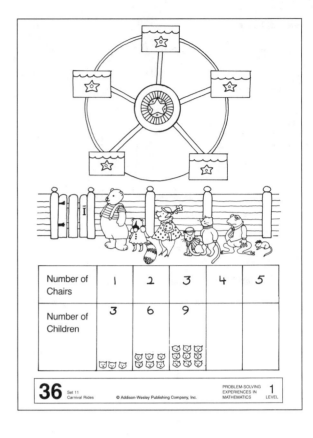

- How many counters would you put in the first box? (*3*) The second box? (*6*) The third box? (*9*) The fourth box? (*12*)
- By what number do the counters increase each time? (*3*)
- What is 3 more than 12? (*15*) How many children can ride the Ferris wheel at one time? (*15*)

STRATEGY ASSESSMENT IDEAS

Listen and watch as students work to see if they

- place items correctly in the table
- use a pattern to correctly extend the table
- interpret the table to arrive at the correct answer
- use manipulatives appropriately

Solution

Complete a Table/Look for a Pattern/Use Manipulatives

Students should use counters on top of the table to show the number of children.

Number of Chairs	1	2	3	4	5
Number of Children	3	6	9	12	15

Pattern: The number of children increases by 3 each time.

The Ferris wheel can hold 15 children at one time.

Related Problems: *43, 24, 23, 20, 19*

Problem Extensions

1. Suppose only 2 adults can sit in each chair. How many adults can ride the Ferris wheel at one time? (*10*)
2. Suppose there are 6 chairs on the Ferris wheel instead of 5. Now how many children can ride on the Ferris wheel? (*18*)

SET 12

A New Year's Day Parade

Hooray! Hooray! There is going to be a parade on Saturday, and Mr. Kamita has promised to take his children, Wendy and Ryan, to see it. The parade will be part of the New Year's Day celebration.

Ryan reads in the newspaper that the parade will have the marching bands from the two high schools in town, people riding horses, clowns riding teeny-tiny tricycles, some TV and movie stars, fire engines, beautiful floats decorated with colorful flowers, and lots and lots of balloons. Mr. Kamita tells Wendy and Ryan that they will have to get up very early on the day of the parade so they can be there in time to get a good place to watch the parade.

Discussion Questions

1. What did Mr. Kamita promise his children? (*to take them to the parade*)
2. What is a float? (*a low cart on wheels that carries people and flowers and displays in a parade*)
3. Why are Wendy and Ryan going to get up very early on the day of the parade? (*so they can get there in time to get a good place to watch the parade*)
4. Have you even been to a parade? Were there a lot of people?

45 SKILL ACTIVITY

Tell a Subtraction Question for a Story

Story A
In the Fairview High School Marching Band, there are 6 drummers and 8 trumpet players.

Possible Question for Story A
How many more trumpet players than drummers are in the band? (2)

Story B
During the parade, a clown came by who was selling balloons and flags. Wendy bought a balloon. She gave the clown 10¢, but balloons only cost 7¢.

Possible Question for Story B
How much money did Wendy get back? (3¢)

TEACHING ACTIONS

1. Read and discuss Story A.
2. Ask students to tell a question that can be answered using subtraction.
3. Repeat for Story B.

46 ONE-STEP PROBLEM

The New Year's Day parade will begin at the corner of Oak and First Streets and travel 10 blocks. After the parade has gone 6 blocks, how many more blocks will it have to go?

MATERIALS
blocks (10 per student)

Understanding the Problem
- What is this story about? (*a parade*)
- Where does the parade begin? (*at the corner of Oak and First*)
- What is a block? (*the distance between 2 cross streets*)
- How far does the parade march? (*10 blocks*)
- What question do we want to answer? (*how far the parade has to go after it has gone 6 blocks*)

Solving the Problem
- Do you know the total distance for the parade? (*yes, 10 blocks*)
- Do you know part of the total distance the parade has marched? (*yes, 6 blocks*)
- To find the other part of the total distance, should you add or subtract? (*subtract*) Which numbers? (*subtract 6 from 10*)

Use Manipulatives
- With the counters, show how many blocks long the parade will be.
- How can you show with counters how many blocks the parade has gone so far? (*take away 6 blocks*)

Solution
Choose the Operation/Use Manipulatives

$10 - 6 = 4$ or $\begin{array}{r} 10 \\ -\ 6 \\ \hline 4 \end{array}$

The parade has 4 more blocks to go.

Problem Extension
Suppose the parade has only marched 3 blocks. How many more blocks does it have to go? (*10 – 3 = 7*)

47 > PROCESS PROBLEM

When the Oakview High School band marched by, Ryan noticed that all the drummers were marching in a row. Each drummer was playing either a large drum or a small drum. He could see all but 2 of the drummers, but after watching them for a while, he saw that they were lined up in a pattern. To find what kind of drums the other 2 drummers were playing, finish the pattern.

MATERIALS

red and blue crayons or markers

Understanding the Problem

- What was the name of the band that marched past Ryan? (*Oakview High School band*)
- How were the drummers marching? (*in a row*)
- What kinds of drums were the drummers playing? (*large or small*)
- Could Ryan see all of the drummers? (*no, he could not see 2*)
- What is a pattern?
- What do we want to find out about the drummers? (*the kinds of drums the last 2 were playing*)

Solving the Problem

- What size drum is the first drummer playing? The second drummer? (*see Blackline Master 38*)
- Is the second drum different from the first drum? (*no*)
- Repeat for drums 3 and 2, 4 and 3, and so on.
- Color all the small drums blue and all the large drums red. What color will the next drum be? (*blue*)

Which comes next?

Solution

Look for a Pattern

The next drummer has a small (blue) drum and the last drummer has a large (red) drum. The pattern is 2 small, 1 large, 2 small, 1 large, and so on.

Related Problems: 44, 43, 24, 23, 20

Problem Extension

Suppose there were one more drummer. What size drum would that drummer have? (*small*)

STRATEGY ASSESSMENT IDEAS

Listen and watch as students work to see if they

- describe the pattern formed by the large and small drums
- extend the pattern correctly
- use the pattern to arrive at the answer

48 PROCESS PROBLEM

Wendy liked the clowns best of all. She noticed that some clowns were round and some were thin, and some had happy faces and some had sad faces. After the parade was over, the clowns lined up in a pattern so Wendy could take their picture. Two clowns didn't want to have their picture taken. Which 2 clowns were they? To find out, finish the pattern for 2 more clowns.

Understanding the Problem

- What did Wendy like best about the parade? (*the clowns*)
- What different kinds of clowns were there? (*round, thin, happy, sad*)
- What did Wendy do after the parade was over? (*took the clowns' picture*)
- Did all of the clowns line up to be in Wendy's picture? (*no*) Why? (*they didn't want their picture taken*)
- What are we trying to find out about the 2 missing clowns? (*what they look like*)

Solving the Problem

- Look at the row of clowns at the top of the page. How is the second clown different from the first clown? (*happy*) Third from the second? (*round and sad*)
- What kind of face does the clown on each side of a sad clown have? (*happy*)
- How does any clown differ from the clowns on each side? (*the clowns on either side of any particular clown have the opposite expression from that clown*)
- Do thin clowns always have a thin clown next to them? (*yes*) Do round clowns always have a round clown next to them? (*yes*)

Solution

Look for a Pattern

Pattern: sad thin, happy thin, sad round, happy round, sad thin, happy thin, and so on.

The last 2 clowns are: sad round, happy round.

Related Problems: 47, 44, 43, 24, 23

Problem Extension

Suppose there were one more clown. What kind of clown would this be? (*sad, thin*)

STRATEGY ASSESSMENT IDEAS

Listen and watch as students work to see if they

- describe the pattern formed by the clowns
- extend the pattern correctly
- use the pattern to arrive at the answer

SET 13

At the Pond

On the Miller's farm is a large pond. Every day many different animals come to the pond to take a bath and have a drink of water. One morning a mother duck with her 5 baby ducklings following her came down to the pond for a swim. While they were swimming, a mother moose and her calf stopped by to get a drink of cool water. Later in the day a deer with very long antlers walked to the pond to cool off by taking a drink and getting in the water.

Animals aren't they only ones that enjoy the pond. The Miller twins, Mark and Marcy, like to visit the pond whenever they can. Mark likes to go fishing, and Marcy likes to swim whenever the weather is warm. But the most fun of all is in the winter! When winter comes, the pond freezes and the twins and their friends go ice skating.

Discussion Questions

1. Who was following the mother duck to the pond? (*her ducklings*) How many ducklings were there? (5)
2. What does it mean to say Mark and Marcy are twins?
3. If you had a pond near your house, what would you like to do at the pond?
4. What happens to the pond in the winter? (*it freezes*)
5. What other animals might enjoy the Miller's pond?

49 SKILL ACTIVITY

Given a Picture, Tell a Subtraction Question

Picture A

In this picture of the pond, the mother duck is swimming and 3 of 5 ducklings are also swimming. The other 2 ducklings are just coming out of the pond onto the shore. (see Blackline Master 41)

Possible Questions for Picture A

How many more ducklings are in the pond than are out of the pond? (2)

Picture B

In this picture of 6 children, 4 are skating and 2 are sitting on the edge of the pond putting on ice skates. (see Blackline Master 41)

Possible Questions for Picture B

Are there more children skating or sitting? (*skating*) How many more? (2)

TEACHING ACTIONS

1. Show and discuss Picture A.
2. Ask students to tell a question that can be answered using subtraction.
3. Repeat for Picture B.
4. (*optional*) Have students answer their questions.

50 ONE-STEP PROBLEM

Marcy went fishing in the pond on Friday and Saturday. On Friday she caught 4 fish and on Saturday she caught 7 fish. How many more fish did she catch on Saturday than on Friday?

MATERIALS

counters (10 per student)

Understanding the Problem

- On what days did Marcy go fishing? (*Friday and Saturday*)
- How many fish did she catch on Friday? (*4*)
- How many fish did she catch on Saturday? (*7*)
- On which day did she catch more fish, Friday or Saturday? (*Saturday*)
- What are we trying to find? (*how many more fish Marcy caught on Saturday than on Friday*)

Solving the Problem

- If you caught 3 fish on Monday and 2 fish on Tuesday, how many more fish did you catch on Monday? (*1*) Do you add or subtract to find the solution? (*subtract*)
- Are you trying to find how many fish Marcy caught in all? (*no*)
- Draw a picture of the 4 fish Marcy caught on Friday and a picture of the 7 fish she caught on Saturday. How many more fish do you have for Saturday than Friday? (*3*)
- Do you use addition or subtraction to solve this problem? (*subtraction*)

Use Manipulatives

- Use counters to show the fish Marcy caught on Friday and counters to show the fish she caught on Saturday. How many more counters are there for Saturday than Friday? (*3*)

Solution

Draw a Picture

$7 - 4 = 3$ or $\begin{array}{r} 7 \\ -4 \\ \hline 3 \end{array}$

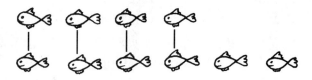

Marcy caught 2 more fish on Saturday than on Friday.

Related Problem: 46

Problem Extensions

1. Suppose Marcy caught 5 fish on Friday and 9 fish on Saturday. How many more fish did she catch on Saturday than on Friday? (*4*)
2. While Marcy was fishing, she saw 4 ducks swimming in the pond and 7 rabbits playing by the pond. How many more rabbits did she see than ducks? (*3*)

Note: The problem and the extension are comparison subtraction stories.

51 PROCESS PROBLEM

Mark and his 2 friends, Ellen and Phil, went fishing at the pond one fine sunny day. Mark had the longest fishing pole. Ellen's fishing pole was longer than Phil's. Who had the shortest fishing pole?

Understanding the Problem

- How many children went fishing? (*3*)
- What did they fish with? (*fishing poles*)
- Were all the fishing poles the same length? (*no*)
- Who had the longest fishing pole? (*Mark*)
- Was Ellen's fishing pole longer or shorter than Phil's? (*longer*)
- What are we trying to find? (*who has the shortest pole*)

Solving the Problem

- Can Ellen's fishing pole be shorter than Phil's? (*no, hers was longer than Phil's*)
- Can you draw Ellen's fishing pole? Is it shorter than Mark's? (*it should be*)
- Can you draw Phil's fishing pole? Is it shorter than Ellen's? (*it should be*) Is it shorter than Mark's? (*yes*)

Note: Some students may get confused about the length of the fishing lines and hooks. Encourage students to keep the right ends of the fishing poles aligned and to not worry about the length of the fishing lines and hooks.

Solution

Use Logical Reasoning/Draw a Picture

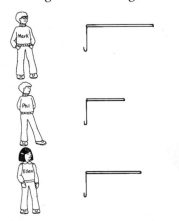

Phil had the shortest fishing pole.

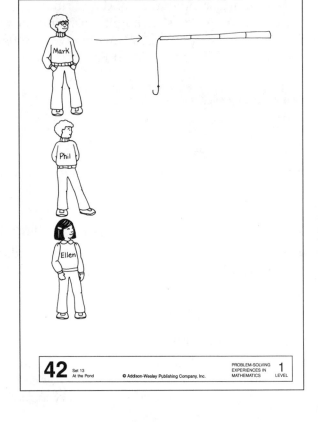

Related Problems: 39, 36, 35, 32, 31

Problem Extension

Suppose Mark had used the medium-size fishing pole instead of the longest. Who would have used the longest fishing pole if Ellen's was still longer than Phil's? (*Ellen*)

STRATEGY ASSESSMENT IDEAS

Listen and watch as students work to see if they

- draw appropriate pictures
- correctly use all conditions given in the problem
- arrive at correct conclusions through reasoning

52 > PROCESS PROBLEM

Mark and Marcy found 5 big green frogs. They named the frogs Freddie, Liz, Becky, Al, and Rose. The twins decided to let the frogs go near the pond and see which frog would get to the pond the fastest. Becky got to the pond first. Rose was the slowest. Al went in the pond behind Freddie, and Freddie reached the pond after Liz. Who reached the pond second? Third? Fourth?

MATERIALS

1" or 2" construction-paper squares or tiles (5 per group)

Understanding the Problem

- What did Mark and Marcy find? (*frogs*)
- How many frogs did they find? (*5*)
- Which frog was fastest? (*Becky; she reached the pond first*)
- Which frog was slowest? (*Rose*)
- Did Freddie reach the pond behind Al? (*no*)
- Which frog did Al go behind? (*Freddie*)

Solving the Problem

- Which frog reached the pond first? (*Becky*)
- Which frog reached the pond last? (*Rose*)
- Where does Liz's name belong? (*see solution*)
- Where should you put Al's name? Freddie's name?

Use Manipulatives

- Use the papers with the frogs' names to help solve the problem. Write the frogs' names on the paper squares, one name to a square.
- Where should you put the paper with Becky's name? (*beside the top frog*)

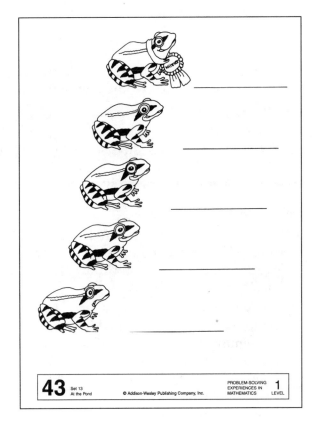

- Where should you put Rose's name? (*beside the bottom frog*)
- Where does Liz's name belong? (*under Becky's*) Why? (*she was second*)
- Where should you put Al's name? Freddie's name? (*see solution*)
- Write the frogs' names in the correct places.

▶ *turn the page*

STRATEGY ASSESSMENT IDEAS

Listen and watch as students work to see if they

- use paper or draw pictures to keep track of their reasoning
- correctly use all conditions given in the problem
- arrive at correct conclusions through reasoning
- use manipulatives appropriately

83

Solution

Use Logical Reasoning/Use Manipulatives

Students should place the papers with the frogs' names in the correct places, then write the names on the lines.

WINNER				*Slowest*
Becky	Liz	Freddie	Al	Rose

Related Problems: 40, 39, 16, 15

Problem Extensions

1. Suppose there were one more frog named Hank. Hank was faster than Rose but slower than Al. Which frog came in second? (*Liz*) Third? (*Freddie*) Fourth? (*Al*) Fifth? (*Hank*)

2. The twins watched the frogs jump. They had a contest to see which frog jumped farthest in one jump. Becky jumped the highest and Rose jumped the lowest. Al jumped higher than Rose but lower than Freddie. Freddie jumped lower than Liz. Which frog came in second in the contest? (*Liz*) Third? (*Freddie*) Fourth? (*Al*)

Note: Some students may not completely understand the concept of ordinal numbers (second, third, fourth).

SET 14

Pizza Party

When Jeff, Mai, Jill, and Tomas are hungry for pizza, the first place they think of is Tony's Pizza. Tony's Pizza sells 4 sizes of pizza—small, medium, large, and jumbo. When you order a pizza at Tony's, you can have any of 5 toppings: sausage, pepperoni, green pepper, onion, and mushroom. In fact, if you want, you can choose 2, 3, 4, or all 5 toppings to put on your pizza.

Tomas's dad owns Tony's Pizza. He prepares the pizza dough for cooking. One day Tomas brought Jeff, Mai, and Jill with him to watch his dad make pizzas. After watching Tomas's dad for a while, they all agreed that making a pizza would be a lot of fun but very hard.

The boys and girls decided to have a pizza party and invite all their friends. Tomas was in charge of getting enough pizza for everyone. Jeff and Mai were in charge of sending party invitations to their friends. Jill's job was to buy napkins, paper plates, and plastic forks.

Discussion Questions

1. Do you like pizza? What is your favorite kind of pizza?
2. How many sizes of pizza does Tony's Pizza sell? *(4)*
3. What topping can you get for a pizza at Tony's? *(sausage, pepperoni, green pepper, onion, mushroom)*
4. Can you order sausage, onions, and mushrooms *(or various other combinations)* for your pizza? *(yes)*
5. What is one thing Tomas's dad does at Tony's? *(prepares the pizza dough)*
6. Have you ever seen someone make a pizza? *(show picture)*
7. Why did Jill buy napkins, paper plates, and plastic forks? *(for the pizza party)*
8. If you could make your own pizza, what would you put on it?

53 SKILL ACTIVITY

Tell the Operation

Problem A
Tomas wanted to buy a lot of different kinds of pizzas for the pizza party. He bought 6 medium pizzas and 5 large pizzas. The medium pizzas had sausage topping. The large pizzas had green peppers. How many pizzas did he buy altogether?

Problem B
Jeff was very hungry, so he ate 9 pieces of pizza. Mai wasn't as hungry. She ate 4 fewer pieces of pizza than Jeff ate. How many pieces of pizza did Mai eat?

Notes
1. The objective for Problem A is to help students recognize that addition is the operation used when you join sets of objects. The objective for Problem B is to help students see that subtraction can be used when 2 sets of objects are being compared to find which has more.
2. It is not a good idea to emphasize key phrases such as *in all* and *how many more* to help students decide which operations to use. The focus should be on joining (*putting together*) for addition and comparing (*to decide which is more*) for subtraction.

TEACHING ACTIONS
1. Read and discuss Problem A.
2. Ask students which operation is needed to solve Problem A. Discuss how the action in the story tells which operation is needed.
3. Repeat for Problem B.
4. (*optional*) Have students solve each problem.

54 ONE-STEP PROBLEM

Tomas's dad made a large mushroom pizza and a medium mushroom pizza for the pizza party. On the large pizza he put 24 slices of mushroom and some green peppers. On the medium pizza he put 13 slices of mushroom and nothing else. How many slices of mushroom did Tomas's dad put on the 2 pizzas?

MATERIALS
counters (50 per student)

Understanding the Problem

- What size pizzas did Tomas's dad make? (*large and medium*)
- What did he put on the large pizza? (*mushrooms and green peppers*)
- How many slices of mushroom did he put on the large pizza? (*24*)
- How many slices of mushroom did he put on the medium pizza? (*13*)
- Was anything else put on the medium pizza besides mushrooms? (*no*)

Solving the Problem

- Are you trying to find how many more slices of mushroom were on the large pizza than the medium pizza? (*no*) What are you trying to find? (*how many slices of mushroom were on both pizzas*)
- If one pizza had 4 slices of mushrooms and another had 2 slices of mushroom, how many slices of mushroom would there be on both pizzas? (*6*) How did you figure out there would be 6 slices?

Use Manipulatives

- Use counters to show the number of slices of mushroom on one pizza. Use counters to show the number of slices of mushroom on the other pizza.
- Put the groups together to find the total number of mushroom slices.

Solution
Choose the Operation/Use Manipulatives

24 + 13 = 37 slices of mushroom

or

$$\begin{array}{r} 24 \\ + 13 \\ \hline 37 \text{ slices of mushroom} \end{array}$$

Tomas's dad put a total of 37 slices of mushroom on the 2 pizzas.

Related Problems: 42, 38

Problem Extensions

1. How many more slices of mushroom were on the large pizza than on the medium pizza? (*24 – 13 = 11 more slices*)
2. A jumbo pizza has 35 slices of mushroom. A large pizza has 24 slices of mushroom. Which has more, the jumbo pizza or the large pizza? (*jumbo*) How many more? (*35 – 24 = 11 more slices*)

55 ▶ PROCESS PROBLEM

Tony's Pizza gives prizes for people who buy certain pizzas. If you buy a large pizza, you get a cap for a prize—either red or blue. If you buy a jumbo pizza, you get a T-shirt for a prize—either orange or green. Elena bought a large pizza and a jumbo pizza so she was given her choice of a cap and a shirt. How many ways can she put the colors together if she wore one cap and one shirt?

MATERIALS

orange, green, red, and blue counters (3 of each color per group); crayons or markers in the same colors

Understanding the Problem

- What prize do you win if you buy a large pizza? (*a cap*)
- What colors are the caps? (*red and blue*) Color the caps Tony is holding at the top of your paper.
- What prize do you win if you buy a jumbo pizza? (*a T-shirt*)
- What colors are the T-shirts? (*orange and green*)
- What did Elena buy? (*a large pizza and a jumbo pizza*)
- What prizes did she win? (*a cap and a T-shirt*)

Solving the Problem

- If you wear a red cap, what color T-shirt could you wear? (*orange or green*)
- If you wear a blue cap, what color T-shirt could you wear? (*orange or green*)

Use Manipulatives

- Use the counters to show the caps and shirts. What color counter could be placed on the first cap? (*blue or red*)
- What color shirt? (*orange or green*) Now pick a different color cap and T-shirt. Continue until you can't think of any more combinations.

STRATEGY ASSESSMENT IDEAS

Listen and watch as students work to see if they

- can show one hat and T-shirt combination
- organize entries in the list
- list all possible entries
- use manipulatives appropriately

Solution

Make an Organized List/Use Manipulatives

Students should place the counters on the caps and T-shirts to find the 4 possible combinations.

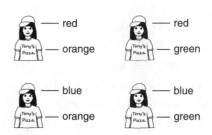

Related Problems: 27, 27, 4, 3

Problem Extension

Suppose Elena had a choice of 3 colors of caps—red, blue, and purple. How many different ways could she wear one color cap and one color T-shirt? (*6*)

88

56 PROCESS PROBLEM

Tomas wanted to get extra toppings on one pizza. The toppings were sausage, pepperoni, green pepper, onion, and mushroom. Tomas paid 14¢ for 3 different extra toppings. Which toppings did he get?

MATERIALS

counters (20 per group)

Understanding the Problem

- What is a topping for a pizza?
- What toppings were there to choose from? (sausage, pepperoni, green pepper, onion, mushroom)
- How much does pepperoni cost? (5¢)
- Which topping cost 3¢? (onion)
- How many extra toppings did Tony buy? (3)
- How much did he pay for the 3 toppings? (14¢)

Solving the Problem

- Could Tomas have bought 1 sausage and 2 mushroom toppings? (no, he bought 3 different toppings)
- Could Tomas have bought sausage, pepperoni, and green pepper? (no, he spent 14¢, not 13¢)
- Can you guess which 3 toppings Tomas bought and then add to check you guess? (see solution)

Use Manipulatives

- Use the counters to show 6¢. Stack them on top of the sausage picture.
- How many counters would you stack on top of the pepperoni? (5) The green pepper? (2) Onion? (3) Mushroom? (4)

Solution

Guess and Check/Use Manipulatives

Students should place counters on top of the toppings, then guess and check to find the answer.

- Try 6¢ + 5¢ + 4¢ = 15¢ (*too much*)
- Try 6¢ + 4¢ + 3¢ = 13¢ (*too little*)
- Try 6¢ + 5¢ + 3¢ = 14¢ (*just right*)

Tony bought sausage, pepperoni, and onion.

Related Problems: 40, 39, 16, 15

Problem Extensions

1. Suppose Tomas paid 10¢ for 3 different extra toppings. Which toppings did he buy? (*pepperoni, onion, and green pepper*)
2. Suppose Tomas bought 2 toppings that were the same and 1 topping that was different. Altogether he paid 15¢. What toppings did he buy? (*sausage and onions*)

STRATEGY ASSESSMENT IDEAS

Listen and watch as students work to see if they

- make guesses that indicate an understanding of problem
- use previous guesses to make better guesses
- check guesses using the information given in the problem
- give appropriate reasons for their guesses
- use manipulatives appropriately

Penguins in the Snow

Willie, Tillie, and Millie are penguins. They live near the South Pole in a very cold and icy place with lots of snow, called Antarctica. Penguins are black and white birds. People like the way the penguins waddle back and forth when they walk. An unusual thing about penguins is that although they are birds, they can't fly. Instead, they are very good swimmers.

Because there is always a lot of snow where they live, Willie, Tillie, and Millie like to build "snowpenguins" when they aren't fishing or swimming. One day they worked for hours building a snowpenguin, and when they finished it was the finest and biggest one they had ever made.

Discussion Questions

1. Where are Willie, Millie, and Tillie? (*penguins*)
2. Have you ever seen a picture of penguins? Have you ever seen penguins in a zoo or on TV?
3. Where do penguins live? (*Antarctica*) Can you find Antarctica on a map of the world?
4. Can penguins fly? Can they swim?
5. What did Willie, Millie, and Tillie build? (*a snow-penguin*)
6. Have you ever built a snowperson or a snow-penguin?

57 SKILL ACTIVITY

Choose Missing Data

Problem A
Millie Penguin went fishing on Monday and on Tuesday. How many more fish did she catch on Tuesday than she did on Monday?

Missing Information—Problem A
1. She caught 4 fish on Monday. (*no*)
2. She caught 4 fish on Monday and 5 fish on Tuesday. (*yes*)
3. She caught 1 more fish on Tuesday than on Monday. (*no*)

Problem B
Willie Penguin has 7 sisters. Tillie Penguin has some sisters too. How many more sisters does Willie have than Tillie?

Missing Information—Problem B
1. Tillie has 2 sisters. (*yes*)
2. Willie has 3 brothers and 4 sisters. (*no*)
3. Millie has 2 brothers and 3 sisters. (*no*)

TEACHING ACTIONS
1. Read and discuss Problem A.
2. Ask, "What else do we need to know to solve the problem?"
3. If necessary, give students the choice for missing information one at a time as follows: "Can we find out if we know . . . ?"
4. Repeat for Problem B.

58 ONE-STEP PROBLEM

Willie, Millie, and Tillie thought it would be fun to have a snowball-throwing contest. They decided to make 15 snowballs. How many more snowballs do they still have to make if they stopped for lunch after they made 9 snowballs?

Understanding the Problem

- What did Willie, Millie, and Tillie think would be fun? (*a snowball-throwing contest*)
- How many snowballs did the penguins decide to make? (*15*)
- How many snowballs did the penguins make before lunch? (*9*)

Solving the Problem

- Are you trying to find how many snowballs they made after lunch? (*yes*)
- If they wanted to make 5 snowballs, how many more would they need to make after they had made 3 snowballs? (*2*) Did you subtract to find this out? (*yes*)
- Can you draw a picture of 15 snowballs and mark off the number of snowballs they have already made?
- After they made 9 snowballs, how many more do they need to make to get 15 in all? (*6*)

Note: Encourage students who want to count to find the answer (or count on 9, 10, 11, 12, 13, 14, 15) to decide which operation, addition or subtraction, could be used.

Solution

Choose the Operation

$15 - 9 = 6$ snowballs

or
```
   15
 - 9  (missing addend)
 ___
   6 snowballs
```

or $9 + 6 = 16$

They still need to make 6 snowballs.

Related Problems: 54, 46

Problem Extensions

1. They made 15 snowballs on Monday and 11 snowballs on Tuesday. How many more snowballs did they make on Monday than on Tuesday? (*4*)
2. They made 24 snowballs one morning, but while they were having lunch, 13 snowballs melted. How many snowballs did they still have? (*11 snowballs*)

59 ▸ PROCESS PROBLEM

Paul Penguin is learning how to fish. When he first started fishing he didn't catch many fish, but he improved every day. On day 1 he caught only 1 fish, but on day 2 he caught 4 fish. Complete the table to decide how many fish he caught on day 5.

MATERIALS
counters (35 per pair)

Understanding the Problem
- Was Paul good at fishing when he started? (*no*)
- How many fish did he catch on day 1? (*1*)
- How many fish did he catch on day 2? (*4*)
- How many fish did he catch on day 3? (Use the table.) (*7*)

Solving the Problem
- How many fish did Paul catch on day 4? (*10*)
- How many more fish did he catch on day 2 than day 1? (*3*)
- How many more fish did he catch on day 3 than day 2? (*3*)
- How many more on day 4 than day 3? (*3*)
- Do you see a number pattern?
- If Paul caught 10 fish on day 4 and catches 3 more each new day, how many fish did he catch on day 5? (*13*)

Use Manipulatives
- Use the counters to show the number of fish on the table.
- How many counters should you put on day 1? (*1*) Day 2? (*4*) Day 3? (*7*) Day 4? (*10*) Day 5? (*13*)
- How many more counters did you have to put down each day? (*3*)

Solution
Make a Table/Look for a Pattern/ Use Manipulatives

Day	1	2	3	4	5
Number of Fish Caught	1	4	7	10	13

Students should stack the counters on the table and count them to find the total.

Pattern: Paul catches 3 more fish each day.

Paul caught 13 fish on day 5.

Related Problems: 48, 47, 44, 43, 24

Problem Extensions
1. How many fish did Paul catch on day 6? (*16 fish*)
2. If Paul caught 1 fish on day 1, 3 on day 2, 5 on day 3, and 7 on day 4, how many did he catch on day 5? (*9*) On day 6? (*11*)

STRATEGY ASSESSMENT IDEAS

Listen and watch as students work to see if they
- place items correctly in the table
- use a pattern to correctly extend the table
- interpret the table to arrive at the correct answer
- use manipulatives appropriately

60 > PROCESS PROBLEM

Millie Penguin and her brothers and sister made a large pile of snowballs to use in the big snowball-throwing contest. Unfortunately, because the sun shone brightly every day, some of their snowballs started to melt. Millie noticed that 1 snowball melted on the first day, 2 more melted on the next day, 4 more melted on the next day, and 7 more melted on the day after that. Millie said, "I think there is a number pattern here." Do you see a number pattern? Complete the table, and then decide how many snowballs will melt on days 5 and 6.

MATERIALS

counters (45 per pair)

Day	1	2	3	4	5	6
Number of Snowballs Melted	1	2	4	7		

Understanding the Problem

- Why did Millie and her brothers and sisters make a pile of snowballs? (*for the snowball-throwing contest*)
- What started happening to the snowballs? (*they started melting*)
- Why did they start melting? (*the sun was bright*)
- How many snowballs melted on day 1? (*1*) On day 2? (*2*)
- How many snowballs melted on day 3? (*4*) On day 4? (*7*)
- What is a number pattern?

Solving the Problem

- How many more snowballs melted on day 2 than day 1? (*1*) How many more melted on day 3 than day 2? (*2*) How many more snowballs melted on day 4 than day 3? (*3*) Do you see a pattern? What number comes next: 1, 2, 3, __ ?
- Can you use this counting pattern to find how many snowballs melted on day 5? Day 6? (*see solution*)

Use Manipulatives

- Use the counters to show the number of snowballs. Stack the counters on the table.
- How many counters should you put on day 1? (*1*) Day 2? (*2*) Day 3? (*4*) Day 4? (*7*)
- How many snowballs melted on day 5? (*see solution*)
- How many counters should be placed on the table? (*7 + 4 = 11*)
- How many counters should be placed on day 6? (*11 + 5 = 16*)

▶ *turn the page*

STRATEGY ASSESSMENT IDEAS

Listen and watch as students work to see if they

- place items correctly in the table
- use a pattern to correctly extend the table
- interpret the table to arrive at the correct answer
- use manipulatives appropriately

Solution

Make a Table/Look for a Pattern/Use Manipulatives

Students should place the counters on the table and count them to find the total number of snowballs that melted.

Day	1	2	3	4	5	6
Number of Snowballs Melted	1	2	4	7	11	16

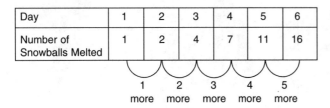

Pattern: One more snowball melts each day than the number that melted the day before: 11 snowballs melted on day 5, and 16 melted on day 6.

Related Problems: 59, 48, 47, 44, 43

Problem Extension

Do you see a pattern in this table? Complete the table and describe the pattern.

Day	1	2	3	4	5	6
Number of Snowballs Melted	3	5	7	9		

SET 16

Happy Valentine's Day

Sidney Squirrel wants to send gifts to all his friends for Valentine's Day. He has decided to send gifts to Susie Squirrel, Ruthie Robin, Bert Beaver, and Willie Penguin (Willie lives at the South Pole). Sidney thinks Valentine's Day is very special because it is a day when you can give presents and cards to your friends to show them how much you like them.

Last year Sidney gave Susie some beautiful flowers—they were carnations—and he gave Ruthie some special bird seed. Sidney sent Bert a very nice card that was shaped like a heart. Inside the card was written, "To my good friend, Bert. Be my Valentine." Because Willie lives in such a cold place (it gets very cold at the South Pole—brrr!!!), Sidney sent him a pair of warm mittens.

Susie, Ruthie, Bert, and Willie were very pleased when they received their gifts. They all felt they were lucky to have a good friend like Sidney.

Discussion Questions

1. Who wants to send gifts to his friends for Valentine's Day? (*Sidney*)
2. Which friends received Valentine's gifts from Sidney last year? (*Susie, Ruthie, Bert, Willie*)
3. Where does Willie Penguin live? (*at the South Pole*)
4. Why is Valentine's Day special?
5. What did Sidney give to Susie? (*carnations*)
6. What was written inside the card Sidney sent to Bert? (*"To my good friend, Bert. Be my Valentine."*)
7. Why did Sidney send Willie a pair of mittens? (*it is cold where Willie lives*)
8. Have you ever given anyone a valentine?

61 SKILL ACTIVITY

Tell Missing Data

Problem A

Sidney gave Susie flowers for Valentine's Day. The flowers were carnations. Five of the carnations were red and the rest were white. How many carnations did Sidney give Susie?

Problem B

Sidney bought a special kind of bird seed for Ruthie. When he went to the store to buy it, he was told that there were 2 kinds of candy. One kind cost 5¢ more than the other. Sidney bought the kind that cost less. How much did he pay for the bird seed?

TEACHING ACTIONS

1. Read and discuss Problem A.
2. Ask students what else they need to know to solve the problem. (*how many white carnations*)
3. (*optional*) Have students make up a reasonable number and solve the problem.
4. Repeat for Problem B.

62. ONE-STEP PROBLEM

Ruthie Robin received 15 valentines from her friends on Valentine's Day, and Bert Beaver received 26 valentines from his friends. How many more valentines did Bert get than Ruthie?

MATERIALS
counters (50 per student)

Understanding the Problem
- Why did Bert and Ruthie received valentines? (*it was Valentine's Day*)
- How many valentines did Ruthie receive? (*15*)
- How many valentines did Bert receive? (*26*)

Solving the Problem
- If Ruthie had 3 valentines and Bert had 5 valentines, how many more did Bert have? (*2*) Did you add 3 and 5 to find how many more Bert had? (*no—subtracted*)
- Can you draw a picture of 15 valentines and 26 valentines and compare them to find the solution? (*see solution*)
- Can you subtract to find the solution? (*yes*)
- If you have 15 valentines, how many more would you need to get to have 26? (*11*)

Use Manipulatives
- Use counters to show how many valentines Ruthie received. Use counters to show how many valentines Bert received.
- How can you compare the groups to find how many more valentines Bert received? (*by using a one-to-one correspondence between groups*)

Solution
Choose the Operation/Use Manipulatives

26 − 15 = 11 valentines   or   26
                                 − 15
                                 ────
                                  11 valentines

Bert had 11 more valentines than Ruthie.

Draw a Picture

11 more valentines

Related Problems: 58, 50, 46

Note: Point out to students that it is faster to choose the operation and do the subtraction than to draw boxes to find the solution.

Problem Extension
If Ruthie received 5 more valentines on the day after Valentine's Day, how many more valentines did Bert have than Ruthie? (*6 more; 11 − 5 = 6*)

63 PROCESS PROBLEM

Ruthie Robin had a Valentine's Day party and invited all her fiends. She baked cookies and made fresh lemonade to give her guests. Her cookies were shaped like hearts, circles, and triangles. She made one more heart cookie than triangle cookies and one more triangle cookie than circle cookies. If she made 5 heart cookies, how many cookies did she make in all?

MATERIALS

counters (5 each of 3 colors per group); crayons or markers

Understanding the Problem

- Which friends did Ruthie invite to her Valentine's Day party? (*all of them*)
- What shapes were the cookies? (*hearts, triangles, and circles*)
- How many more hearts did she bake than triangles? (*1 more*)
- How many more triangles did she bake than circles? (*1 more*)
- How many hearts did she bake? (*5*)

Solving the Problem

- Can you draw more hearts to show how many Ruthie baked? Now, can you draw more triangles to show how many Ruthie baked? Now draw the right number of circles. How many cookies are shown in all?

Use Manipulatives

- Use the counters to show the cookies. Let the red counters be hearts, the blue counters be triangles, and the yellow counters be circles.

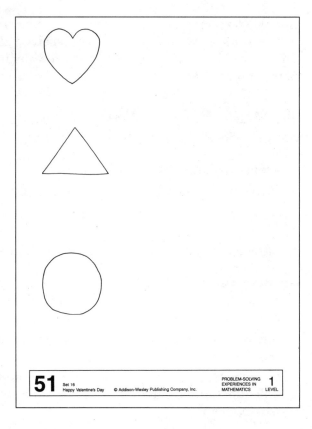

- How many red counters should be placed on the paper? (*5*)
- If Ruthie made one more heart cookie than triangle cookies, how many blue counters should there be? (*4*) If she made one more triangle cookie than circle cookies, how many yellow counters will there be? (*3*)
- Count all the counters. How many cookies did Ruthie bake in all? (*12*)

STRATEGY ASSESSMENT IDEAS

Listen and watch as students work to see if they

- draw the correct number of each shape
- give appropriate reasons for using the numbers of counters they used

Solution

Draw a Picture/Use Manipulatives

Students should place the counters on the paper to show the cookies.

She made 12 cookies in all.

Related Problems: 51, 36, 35, 12, 11

Problem Extension

Suppose Ruthie made 2 more heart cookies than triangle cookies and 2 more triangle cookies than circle cookies. If she made 7 heart cookies, how many cookies did she make in all? (*15*)

64 PROCESS PROBLEM

Susie Squirrel was puzzled! She got valentines from 3 of her good friends, but she couldn't remember who sent which valentine. When she asked them, Dale, her chipmunk friend, said, "I didn't send you the heart." Waldo Woodpecker said, "I sent you the one shaped like a star." Her cat friend, Fluffy, said, "I don't remember which card I sent you." Help Susie figure out who sent her the 3 cards.

Understanding the Problem

- What does it mean to be puzzled? (*confused, uncertain*)
- Why was Susie puzzled? (*she couldn't remember who sent her which card*)
- How many of Susie's friends sent her valentines? (*3*)
- What did Dale the Chipmunk tell her? (*"I didn't send you the heart"*)
- Which valentine did Waldo send her? (*the one shaped like a star*)
- Did Fluffy remember which card she sent Susie? (*no*)

Solving the Problem

- Which valentine did Waldo send Susie? (*star*) What valentine could Fluffy have sent Susie? (*the heart or the flower*) Could Dale have sent her the heart? (*no*) Then which valentine did Dale send her? (*the flower*) Which valentine did Fluffy send her? (*the heart*)
- Draw a line from Waldo to the valentine he sent. Should you draw a line from Dale to the heart? (*no*) Where should you draw a line from Dale? (*to the flower*) Now, where will you draw the line from Fluffy? (*to the heart*)

Solution

Use Logical Reasoning/Draw a Picture

Related Problems: 52, 51, 39, 36, 35

Problem Extension

(Add a butterfly to the column of card pictures and a penguin to the column of animal pictures.) One Valentine's Day, Susie Squirrel received cards from 4 of her good friends, but she couldn't remember who sent which card. Millie Penguin said, "I sent you a card shaped like something that flies." Dale Chipmunk said, "I sent you a card shaped like a star." Fluffy Cat said, "My card was not shaped like a flower." Waldo Woodpecker said, "I will not tell you which card I sent." Which card did Waldo send? (*flower*)

STRATEGY ASSESSMENT IDEAS

Listen and watch as students work to see if they

- draw lines or record in some way that go together
- correctly use all conditions given in the problem
- arrive at correct conclusions through reasoning

More Vegetables

The carrot gardens Ricky, Mary, and Billy Rabbit planted last year were a success! They had so many carrots, they even gave some away to their friends and neighbors.

Ricky and Billy planted only carrots in their gardens last spring. Since carrots are their favorite food, they decided not to use up garden space for any other vegetables. Mary likes carrots too but she also likes tomatoes. Mary planted carrots in her garden last year, but she used some of her garden to plant tomatoes. This year she wants to plant tomatoes and carrots again.

Even though carrots are Ricky's and Billy's favorite vegetables, they did get a little tired of eating them. One day Ricky ate so many carrots that that night he dreamed he turned into one! Ricky and Billy want to plant carrots again this spring, but they both decided they would plant some other vegetables too—just in case!

Discussion Questions

1. Why did the rabbits think that their carrot gardens were a success? (*they had so many they could give some away*)
2. Did all three children plant the same vegetables in their gardens last spring? (*no*)
3. Why did Ricky and Billy get tired of carrots? (*because that's the only vegetable they planted*)
4. Have you ever gotten tired of eating a particular kind of food?
5. Ricky and Billy planted some vegetables besides carrots—just in case. "Just in case" what? (*they get tired of carrots again*)
6. If you planted a garden, what vegetables would you be sure to plant? What vegetables would you not want to plant?

65 SKILL ACTIVITY

Tell a Story Problem

Setting
Ricky, Mary, and Billy Rabbit help each other in their gardens.

Number Sentence A
8 + 3 = ?

Number Sentence B
5 + 5 = ?

Possible Story for Number Sentence A
Ricky, Mary, and Billy Rabbit worked in their gardens all weekend. On Saturday they worked 8 hours. On Sunday they worked 3 hours. How many hours altogether did they work in their gardens?

Possible Story for Number Sentence B
Billy planted 2 rows of carrots today. Each row had 5 carrots in it. How many carrots did he plant in all?

Note: Be sure students end their stories with questions that call for the use of addition.

TEACHING ACTIONS

1. Read the story setting.
2. Have students tell a story problem that would be solved using Number Sentence A.
3. Repeat for Number Sentence B.
4. (*optional*) Have students solve their story problems.

66 ONE-STEP PROBLEM

Mary Rabbit has 2 favorite types of vegetables: carrots and tomatoes. Last spring she planted 11 tomato plants. She had so many tomatoes last summer that she had to give baskets of them away. This spring Mary has decided to plant only 7 tomato plants. How many more plants did she plant last spring than she is going to plant this spring?

Understanding the Problem

- What are Mary's 2 favorite types of food? (*carrots and tomatoes*)
- What did Mary plant 11 of last spring? (*tomato plants*)
- What happened when she did this? (*she had too many tomatoes to eat*)
- Did she plant 11 tomato plants again this spring? (*no*) How many did she plant? (*7*)
- What are we trying to find? (*how many more tomato plants Mary planted last spring than she will plant this spring*)

Solving the Problem

- If you had 3 apples and 2 oranges, how many more apples than oranges do you have? (*1*) Do you add or subtract to find that answer? (*subtract*)
- Are you trying to find the total number of plants for the 2 summers? (*no*) Do you use addition to solve this problem? (*no*)
- Use counters (or draw a picture) to show the 11 plants planted last spring. Now show the 7 planted this spring. (*see solution*)

Solution

Choose the Operation

$11 - 7 = 4$ rows   or $\begin{array}{r} 11 \\ -7 \\ \hline 4 \end{array}$

Draw a Picture

○○○○○○○○○○○
○○○○○○○

Mary planted 4 more tomato plants last spring.

Note: The original problem is a comparison subtraction story problem.

Related Problems: 62, 58, 50, 46

Problem Extensions

1. Suppose Mary planted only 5 plants this spring instead of 7. How many more did she plant last spring? (*6*)
2. Mary has only carrots and tomatoes in her garden this summer. She has 6 rows of carrots and 3 rows of tomatoes. How many rows of vegetables does she have in her garden? (*9*)

67 PROCESS PROBLEM

Every morning in the summer, Billy Rabbit gets out of bed as soon as the sun starts to shine. After eating breakfast, he puts on his garden clothes and goes outside to look at his vegetables. Billy has 2 garden shirts; one is red and the other is green. He also has 2 pairs of shorts he wears to work in the garden; one is blue and the other is yellow. How many ways can Billy wear one of the shirts and one of the shorts?

MATERIALS

red, yellow, green, and blue counters (at least 4 of each color per group)

Understanding the Problem

- What does Billy do right after breakfast? (*puts on his garden clothes and goes out to check his vegetables*)
- What are garden clothes?
- How many garden shirts does Billy have? (2) Can you point to them on your paper? What colors are his shirts? (*red and green*) Color Billy's shirts that are hanging from the tree. Now color his shorts on the tree.

Solving the Problem

- Name one shirt Billy can wear. (*red or green*)
- If Billy wears that shirt, name one pair of shorts he can wear with it. (*blue or yellow*)
- If Billy wears the red shirt, name one color shorts he could wear. (*blue or yellow*)
- The red shirt and blue shorts is one way. Can you find another way?

Use Manipulatives

- Use the counters to show the shirts and shorts.
- Place the red counter on the paper. What color counter could go with the red? (*blue or yellow*)
- Place the green counter on the paper. What color counter can go with green? (*blue or yellow*)
- How many combinations are possible? (4)

STRATEGY ASSESSMENT IDEAS

Listen and watch as students work to see if they

- give one shirt-and-shorts combination
- organize entries in the list
- list all possible entries
- use manipulatives appropriately

Solution

Make an Organized List, Use Manipulatives

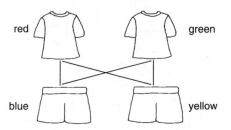

Students should place the counters on the paper to find the 4 possible combinations.

Related Problems: 55, 36, 35, 28, 27

Problem Extension

Suppose Billy also had a purple shirt. Now there are 6 different ways to put one shirt with one of the pairs of shorts. Can you find the 6 ways?

68 PROCESS PROBLEM

Ricky saw an advertisement in the newspaper that the Country Store had a sale on vegetable seeds. Ricky hurried over to the store and bought one scoop of each of the seeds he wanted. Which seeds did Ricky buy?

Note: Be sure students can identify the labels on the seed bins on Blackline Master 55.

MATERIALS

counters (30 per pair)

Understanding the Problem

- What is an advertisement in a newspaper?
- What is on sale at the Country Store? (*vegetable seeds*)
- How many kinds of seeds are in the boxes? (*6*)
- How much do carrot seeds cost? (*7¢ a scoop*)
- What kind of seeds costs 2¢ a scoop? (*celery*)
- How many kinds of seeds did Ricky buy? (*3*)
- Are they all the same seeds? (*no, they are different*)
- How much did he pay altogether? (*11¢*)

Solving the Problem

- Could Ricky have bought only tomato seeds and carrot seeds? (*no, he bought 3 kinds of seeds*)
- Could Ricky have bought lettuce seeds, celery seeds, and cabbage seeds? (*no, he spent 11¢, not 10¢*)
- Can you guess which 3 kinds of seeds Ricky bought and then add to check your guess? (*see solution*)

Use Manipulatives

- Use the counters to show the money amounts in the table.
- How many counters should you put on the carrot seeds? (*7*) On the lettuce seeds? (*3*) Celery seeds? (*2*) Tomato seeds? (*6*) Cabbage seeds? (*5*) Radish seeds? (*4*)
- Can you guess which kinds of seeds Ricky bought and then add the counters to check your guess? (*see solution*)

STRATEGY ASSESSMENT IDEAS

Listen and watch as students work to see if they

- make guesses that indicate an understanding of the problem
- use previous guesses to make better guesses
- check guesses using the information given in the problem
- give appropriate reasons for their guesses
- use manipulatives appropriately

Solution

Guess and Check/Use Manipulatives

Students should stack the counters on top of the money amounts in the table, then add to find the answer.

- Try 3¢ + 2¢ + 4¢ = 9¢ (*too low*)
- Try 5¢ + 4¢ + 2¢ = 12¢ (*too high*)
- Try 6¢ + 3¢ + 2¢ = 11¢ (*correct*)
- Try 5¢ + 4¢ + 2¢ = 11¢ (*correct*)

Ricky bought tomato seeds, lettuce seeds, and celery seeds; or Ricky bought cabbage seeds, radish seeds, and celery seeds.

Note: There are two valid solutions.

Related Problems: 56, 40, 39, 16, 15

Problem Extensions

1. Suppose Ricky paid 9¢ for 3 different kinds of seeds. Which ones did he buy? (*lettuce, celery, radish*)

2. Suppose Ricky bought 2 scoops of one kind of seed and 1 scoop of another kind and paid 10¢ altogether. What seeds did he buy? (*lettuce and radish; or radish and celery*)

More Pets

One reason most children think Mr. Cummings' pet store is the best is that he lets them play with the animals. Of course, they must handle the animals very gently. Also, Mr. Cummings says that some animals, such as snakes, get scared very easily and might hurt someone. So he doesn't let people play with all the animals in the store.

Next to the puppies and kittens, most of the children who visit Mr. Cummings' store like to play with the hamsters and gerbils. The children like to touch their fur, and they love to watch the hamsters and gerbils run around in their cages.

Every time the children come in to Mr. Cummings' store, the first thing they do is ask Mr. Cummings if he has any new animals for them to see. Some of the children look at the new animals and then go home, but most of the children never leave Mr. Cummings' store before they pet the kittens and puppies.

Discussion Questions

1. Why do most children think Mr. Cummings' pet store is the best? (*he lets them play with the animals*)
2. How must the animals be handled? (*very gently*)
3. Why doesn't Mr. Cummings let the children play with all of the animals? (*some animals get scared easily and might hurt someone*)
4. Why do the children like to touch the hamsters' and gerbils' fur?
5. If you went to a pet store, what kind of animal would you want to see first?

69 SKILL ACTIVITY

Tell a Story Problem

Setting

Mr. Cummings' Pet Store has just about every kind of animal you can think of.

Number Sentence A

5 + 6 = ?

Number Sentence B

4 + 4 = ?

Possible Story for Number Sentence A

Mr. Cummings has gold fish and yellow fish in one tank. There are 5 gold fish and 6 yellow fish in the tank. How many fish are in the tank?

Possible Story for Number Sentence B

The cages in the pet store have parakeets in them. There are 4 parakeets in each cage. How many parakeets are in the cages in all?

TEACHING ACTIONS

1. Read the story setting.
2. Have students tell a story problem that would be solved using Number Sentence A.
3. Repeat for Number Sentence B.
4. (*optional*) Have students solve their story problems.

70 ONE-STEP PROBLEM

Mr. Cummings has gerbils and hamsters in his pet store. Some people forget which are the gerbils and which are the hamsters, so Mr. Cummings has a sign on each cage. Right now Mr. Cummings only has 8 gerbils and 12 hamsters. How many more hamsters than gerbils does Mr. Cummings have?

Understanding the Problem

- Why does Mr. Cummings keep signs on the hamster and gerbil cages? (*some people forget which is which*)
- Does Mr. Cummings have some hamsters and gerbils in his store right now? (*yes*)
- How many hamsters does he have? (*12*) How many gerbils? (*8*)
- What are we trying to find out about the hamsters and gerbils? (*how many more hamsters than gerbils there are*)

Solving the Problem

- Are you trying to find the total number of hamsters and gerbils in the store? (*no*) Should you use addition to solve this problem? (*no*)
- If you had 3 hamsters and 2 gerbils, how many more hamsters than gerbils would you have? (*1*) Did you add or subtract to find this answer? (*subtract*)

Solution

Choose the Operation

12 − 8 = 4   or   12
                    − 8
                    ───
                      4

Draw a Picture

○○○○○○○○○○○○ ← 12 hamsters
○○○○○○○○   ← 8 gerbils

There are 4 more hamsters than gerbils in the store.

Note: This is a comparison subtraction story problem.

Related Problems: 66, 62, 58, 50, 46

Problem Extensions

1. Suppose Mr. Cummings sold 6 of the hamsters. How many hamsters would he still have? (*6*)
2. Suppose Mr. Cummings has 10 mice in his store. How many more mice than gerbils does he have? (*2*)

71 ▸ PROCESS PROBLEM

At the front of Mr. Cummings' pet store, right beside the cash register, is a box of dog yummies. You can buy one dog yummy for 3¢. Each additional dog yummy you buy costs 2¢. How much would you have to pay for 5 dog yummies? Finish writing numbers in the table to help you.

MATERIALS

counters (20 of one color and 40 of another color per group)

Understanding the Problem

- What does Mr. Cummings have next to the cash register? (*a box of dog yummies*)
- Do you pay the same for each dog yummy? (*no*) How much do you pay for the first one you buy? (*3¢*) How much do you pay for each additional dog yummy? (*2¢*)
- How many dog yummies do you want to buy? (*5*)

Solving the Problem

- Look at the table. What do the numbers in the top row tell you? (*the number of dog yummies bought*) The bottom row? (*the total cost*)
- How much would you pay for 2 yummies? (*5¢*) How much more is this than what you would pay for 1 yummy? (*2¢ more*)
- How much would you pay for 3 dog yummies? (*7¢*) How much more is this than what you paid for 2 dog yummies? (*2¢ more*)
- Each time you buy another dog yummy, how much more do you pay? (*2¢ more*)
- What is the cost to buy 4 dog yummies? (*9¢*) If you add 2¢ to 7¢, do you get 9¢? (*yes*)

Use Manipulatives

- Use the two colors of counters to show the information given in the table.
- How does the total cost increase each time? (*2¢*) Use counters to show the cost for 4 dog yummies, then 5 dog yummies.

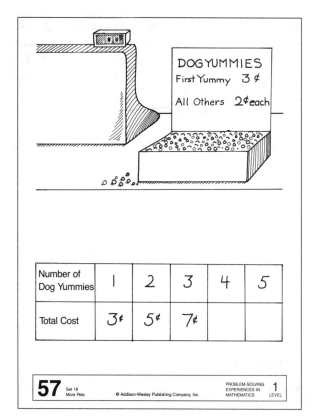

Number of Dog Yummies	1	2	3	4	5
Total Cost	3¢	5¢	7¢		

Solution

Make a Table/Look for a Pattern/Use Manipulatives

Number of Dog Yummies	1	2	3	4	5
Total Cost	3¢	5¢	7¢	9¢	11¢

Pattern: The total cost increases by 2¢ each time. You would pay 11¢ for 5 dog yummies.

Related Problems: 60, 59, 44, 43, 20

Problem Extension

If you paid 13¢, how many dog yummies did you buy? (*6*)

STRATEGY ASSESSMENT IDEAS

Listen and watch as students work to see if they

- place items correctly in the table
- use a pattern to correctly extend the table
- interpret the table to arrive at the correct answer

72 PROCESS PROBLEM

Mr. Cummings has name tags for dogs in two different shapes and two different sizes. When Mr. Cummings puts the name tags on the wall of his store, he hangs them in a certain way. Can you draw the next two name tags Mr. Cummings is going to hang on the wall?

MATERIALS

small and large construction-paper squares and triangles, cut to match the name tags (3 of each shape per group)

Understanding the Problem

- What does Mr. Cummings have in his store? (*name tags for dogs*)
- Are all of the name tags the same? (*no*) How are they different? (*different shapes, different sizes*)
- What shapes are the name tags? (*squares and triangles*)
- What sizes are the name tags? (*large and small*)
- Can you point to a large triangle name tag?
- What are we trying to find? (*which name tags will be placed next on the wall*)

Solving the Problem

- Look at the first two name tags. How are they the same? (*same shape; square*) How are they different? (*first is large, second is small*)
- Look at the next two name tags. How are they the same? (*both triangles*) How are they different? (*first is large, second is small*)
- There are two squares and then two triangles. What shape should the next two shapes be? (*squares*)

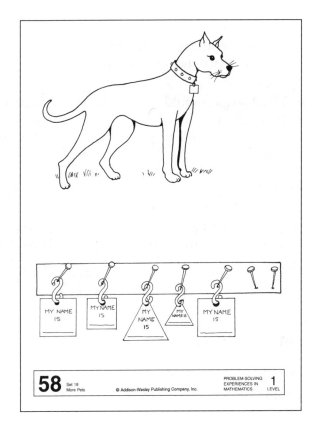

- The shapes are arranged as large, small, large, small, and large. What is the size of the next shape? (*small*)
- Do you see a pattern in the shapes? (*2 squares, 2 triangles, 2 squares, 2 triangles*)
- Do you see a pattern in the sizes? (*large, small, large, small*)

▶ turn the page

STRATEGY ASSESSMENT IDEAS

Listen and watch as students work to see if they

- describe the pattern formed by the shapes
- extend the pattern correctly
- use the pattern to arrive at the answer
- use manipulatives appropriately

115

Use Manipulatives

- Use the paper shapes to find the next shape in the pattern. Place the large square on top of the first tag.
- What shape should come next? (*small square*) Next will be? (*large triangle*) Next? (*small triangle*) Next? (*large square*) Next? (*small square*) Next? (*large triangle*)

Solution

Look for a Pattern/Use Manipulatives

Students should place the paper shapes on top of the tags to help find the next shape in the pattern.

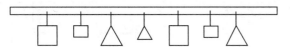

Related Problems: 60, 59, 48, 47, 44

Problem Extensions

1. Suppose the pattern were this:

□ □ △ □ □ __ __

What are the last two shapes? (*triangle, square*)

2. Suppose the pattern were this:

□ △ ○ □ △ ○ □ __ __

What are the last two shapes? (*triangle, circle*)

Sports and Games

Bert Bear and Cindy Bear are twins, and Happy Bear is their older brother. Happy is 2 years older than Bert and Cindy, but the three of them get along so well they almost always play together.

Bert, Cindy, and Happy like all kinds of sports. In the summer their favorite sports are swimming, soccer, and softball. In the winter they all like to ice skate best. Bert and Cindy like to go bowling in the winter, but Happy has never liked bowling. Sometimes he goes along just to watch.

Bert, Cindy, and Happy feel good when they play a game and win. If one bear loses, the others will try to cheer that bear up. Last week they lost a soccer game by only 1 point. Their father told them that they had played a very good team and that they had tried very hard. This made them feel better.

Discussion Questions

1. How are Bert, Cindy, and Happy related? (*brothers and sister*)
2. What do they like to do best in the winter? (*ice skate*)
3. Why might Happy not like bowling?
4. How do they feel when they win? (*good*)
5. How did their father say after they lost a soccer game? (*told them they had played a very good team and they had tried hard*)
6. What is your favorite sport?

73 SKILL ACTIVITY

Tell a Story Problem

Setting

Bert, Cindy, and Happy Bear love to ice skate in the winter.

Number Sentence A

12 − 3 = ?

Number Sentence B

9 − 5 = ?

Possible Story for Number Sentence A

Cindy skated around the lake 12 times. She only fell 3 of the trips around the lake. On how many trips did she not fall down?

Possible Story for Number Sentence B

When Bert, Cindy, and Happy got to the lake, there were 9 bears skating. An hour later, there were only 5 bears skating. How many bears had left?

TEACHING ACTIONS

1. Read the story setting.
2. Have students tell a story problem that would be solved using Number Sentence A.
3. Repeat for Number Sentence B.
4. (*optional*) Have students solve their story problems.

74 ONE-STEP PROBLEM

Every Tuesday night after school, Bert and Cindy went bowling. Happy didn't like to bowl, but he usually went with them to keep the score. Last Tuesday Bert and Cindy each bowled two games. The winner is the bear with the highest total score. Who was the winner last Tuesday?

Understanding the Problem

- Who went bowling? (*Bert and Cindy*)
- What did Happy do? (*kept score*)
- How many games of bowling did Bert and Cindy each play? (*2*)
- What were Bert's scores? (*63 and 35*)
- What were Cindy's scores? (*42 and 53*)
- What was the bear called that had the highest total score? (*the winner*)
- Do you know the total score for Bert or Cindy? (*no*)

Solving the Problem

- What operation should you use to find the total scores? (*addition*)
- Can you write a number sentence to show how to find Bert's total score? (*63 + 35*) What is Bert's total score? (*98*)
- Can you write a number sentence to show how to find Cindy's total score? (*42 + 53*) What is Cindy's total score? (*95*)
- Which number is greater, 98 or 95? (*98*)

Solution

Choose the Operation

```
   63           42
 + 35         + 53
 ----         ----
   98 Bert's total   95 Cindy's total
```

Bert was the winner last Tuesday.

Note: This is the first time students have had to get data from a chart such as this.

Related Problems: 54, 42, 38

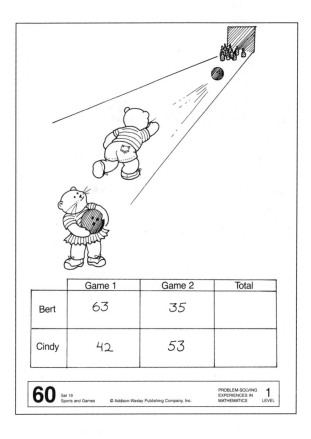

Problem Extensions

1. By how many points did Bert win last Tuesday? (*3*)
2. Suppose Happy had bowled 32 and 56. What would be his total score? (*88*)

119

75 PROCESS PROBLEM

Bert, Cindy, and Happy all play softball and they each have a different color cap. One cap is red, one is blue, and one is green. Cindy's cap is red. Happy doesn't have the blue cap. Who has the green cap?

MATERIALS

red, blue, and green counters (1 of each color per group); red, blue, and green crayons or markers

Understanding the Problem
- What sport do they all play? (*softball*)
- Are their caps the same? (*no, they are different colors*)
- What colors are the caps? (*red, blue, green*)
- Who has a red cap? (*Cindy*)
- What cap doesn't Happy have? (*a blue cap*)
- What are we trying to find? (*who has the green cap*)

Solving the Problem
- Can Bert or Happy have a red cap? (*no, Cindy has the red cap*)
- Can you trace and color Cindy's cap? (*see solution*)
- If Happy doesn't have a blue cap, who has a blue cap? (*Bert*)
- If Cindy's cap is red and Bert's cap is blue, who has the green cap? (*Happy*)

Use Manipulatives
- Use the counters to show the different color caps.
- What color cap does Cindy have? (*red*) Place the red counter next to Cindy.
- If Happy doesn't have the blue cap, who has it? (*Bert*) Where should the blue counter be placed? (*next to Bert*)
- Where should the green counter be placed? (*next to Happy*) Who has the green cap? (*Happy*)

Solution
Use Logical Reasoning/Draw a Picture/Use Manipulatives

Students use counters to show the caps.

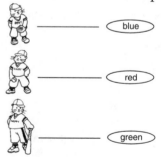

Happy has the green cap.

Related Problems: 67, 64, 63, 52, 51

Problem Extension
Suppose Bert has the red cap and Happy doesn't have the green cap. Who has the blue cap? (*Happy*)

STRATEGY ASSESSMENT IDEAS

Listen and watch as students work to see if they
- show the information given
- correctly use all conditions given in the problem
- arrive at correct conclusions through reasoning
- use manipulatives appropriately

76 PROCESS PROBLEM

Bert, Cindy, and Happy all play soccer for a team called the Rockets. This Saturday they will play a team called the Cowboys. So far, the Cowboys have beaten the Rockets in each of the first 3 games. If both the Rockets and Cowboys continue to score runs as they did in the first 3 games, who will win the fifth game and what will the score be?

Understanding the Problem

- What team do Bert, Cindy, and Happy play soccer for? (*Rockets*)
- What is the name of the other team? (*Cowboys*)
- Which team has won the first 3 games? (*Cowboys*)
- What was the score of the first game? (*5–2*) The second game? (*6–4*) The third game? (*7–6*)
- What are we trying to find? (*which team will win the fifth game and what the score of the game will be*)

Solving the Problem

- How many runs did the Rockets score in the first game? (*2*) The second game? (*4*) The third game? (*6*) How many more runs did the Rockets score in each new game? (*2 more than the previous game*)
- Look at the runs scored by the Rockets. Do you see a pattern in the numbers? (*add 2 each time*)
- Do you see a pattern in the number of runs scored by the Cowboys? (*add 1 each time*)
- How many runs will the Rockets score in game 4? (*8*) The Cowboys in game 4? (*8*) Will one team win? (*no, it will be a tie*)

Solution

Make the Table/Look for a Pattern

	Game 1	Game 2	Game 3	Game 4	Game 5
Rockets	2	4	6	8	10
Cowboys	5	6	7	8	9

The Rockets won the fifth game. The score was 10 to 9.

Note: There are two patterns students must find to solve the problem. This is the first problem in which students have been asked to do this.

	Game 1	Game 2	Game 3	Game 4	Game 5
Rockets	2	4	6		
Cowboys	5	6	7		

Related Problems: 72, 71, 60, 59, 48

Problem Extensions

1. What would the final score be if they played a sixth game? (*Rockets 12, Cowboys 10*)
2. What would the score be for game 5 in the table below? (*Rockets 14, Cowboys 13*)

	Game 1	Game 2	Game 3	Game 4	Game 5
Rockets	2	5	8	11	
Cowboys	5	7	9	11	

STRATEGY ASSESSMENT IDEAS

Listen and watch as students work to see if they

- place items correctly in the table
- use a pattern to correctly extend the table
- interpret the table to arrive at the correct answer

SET 20

All About Dinosaurs

On each school day for the past 2 weeks, Kip's class has spent time learning about dinosaurs. All of the students really like learning about dinosaurs, and each night they tell their families everything they have learned that day.

Kip has learned that there were all different kinds of dinosaurs, and each kind had a name. Brontosaurus, Tyrannosaurus, and Triceratops are the names Kip likes best. He has also learned that some dinosaurs ate trees and plants and some dinosaurs ate meat—fish and birds and even other dinosaurs!

When Kip was 3 years old, his parents took him to a museum to see dinosaur bones. Since Kip is 6 years old now and doesn't remember very much about his visit to the museum, Kip's parents are going to take him to the museum again next Saturday.

Kip has been asking his mother and father a thousand questions about what they will see at the museum. He even asked his parents if they would see a live dinosaur, even though he really knew they wouldn't!

Discussion Questions

1. What is Kip's class learning about? (*dinosaurs*)
2. What has Kip learned about dinosaurs? (*there are different kinds, each kind has a name, and they eat different things*)
3. What is a museum?
4. How old was Kip when he first visited the museum? (*3*)
5. How old is Kip now? (*6*)
6. What questions might Kip have asked his parents about the museum?
7. Why did Kip know they really wouldn't see a live dinosaur at the museum?

77 ▷ SKILL ACTIVITY

Tell a Story Problem

Setting
Kip and his father and mother visited a museum on Saturday.

Number Sentence A
10 – 2 = ?

Number Sentence B
8 – 6 = ?

Possible Story for Number Sentence A
Kip and his parents each had an apple drink at the museum. The drinks cost $2 altogether. How much money should Kip's mother get back if she paid for the drinks with a $10 bill?

Possible Story for Number Sentence B
There were 8 dinosaur skeletons at the museum the last time Kip was there. There were only 6 skeletons when they visited on Saturday. How many dinosaur skeletons were taken away?

TEACHING ACTIONS

1. Read the story setting.
2. Have students tell a story problem that would be solved using Number Sentence A.
3. Repeat for Number Sentence B.
4. (*optional*) Have students solve their story problems.

78 ONE-STEP PROBLEM

The skeletons of two dinosaurs were in one big room. One of the dinosaurs was so big it filled the whole room. It was called a Brontosaurus and it was 64 feet long. The other was a Triceratops. It was only 21 feet long. Kip's father asked Kip how many feet larger the Brontosaurus was than the Triceratops. What was Kip's answer?

Understanding the Problem

- How many dinosaurs were in the room? (*2*)
- Were real live dinosaurs in the room? (*no—skeletons*)
- What was the name of the larger dinosaur? (*Brontosaurus*) How long was it? (*64 feet*)
- What was the name of the shorter dinosaur? (*Triceratops*) How long was it? (*21 feet*)
- What are we trying to find out about these two dinosaurs? (*how much longer the Brontosaurus skeleton is than the Triceratops skeleton*)

Solving the Problem

- Are you trying to find the total lengths of the two dinosaurs? (*no*) Then is addition needed to solve this problem? (*no*)
- If one dinosaur was 6 feet long and another was 4 feet long, how much longer is the longer dinosaur? (*2 feet longer*) Which operation did you use to find the solution? (*subtraction*)
- To compare the lengths to find how much longer one is than the other, should you use the addition or use subtraction? (*subtraction*)

Solution

Choose the Operation

64 − 21 = 43 feet   or   64
                          − 21
                          ────
                            43

The Brontosaurus is 43 feet longer than the Triceratops.

Related Problems: 70, 66, 62, 58, 50

Problem Extensions

1. If the two dinosaurs were placed end to end, how long would they be altogether? (*85 feet*)
2. The Diplodocus is the largest dinosaur known. The largest Diplodocus skeleton ever found was about 87 feet long. How much longer is this Diplodocus than the Brontosaurus? (*23 feet*)

79 PROCESS PROBLEM

The lady who sold Kip's father a map of the museum said that there are 6 different ways to walk from the entrance of the museum to the exit if you walk through only one hallway in each building of the museum. Can you find the 6 different ways to walk through the museum?

Understanding the Problem

- What is a hallway?
- There are two buildings in the museum. Can you point to the first building? (*ENTRANCE building in Blackline Master 64*) How many hallways are in the first building? (*3*) What letters are on the hallways? (*A, B, and C*) What animals are in each hallway? (Note: Discuss with students the meanings of entrance and exit.)
- Can you point to the second building? (*EXIT building*) How many hallways are in the second building? (*2*) What letters are on these hallways? (*D and E*) What animals are in each hallway?
- What does it mean to walk through only one hallway in each building? (*for example—to walk only through hallway B in the first building*)
- How many different ways are there to walk from the entrance to the exit? (*6*)

Solving the Problem

- Pick one hallway in the first building. Now pick one hallway in the second building. Which hallways did you pick?
- If you went through hallway A in the first building, which hallway could you pick in the second building? (*D, for example*) So (for example) A then D would be one way. If you went through A first again, is there another way to go through the second building? (*yes, A then E*)
- Use your finger to trace one way to go from the entrance to the exit. Which two hallways did you go through? Can you trace another way?

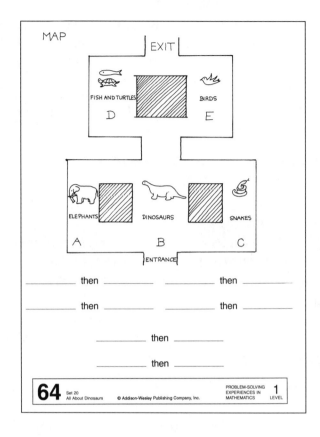

Solution

Make an Organized List

| A then D | B then D | C then D |
| A then E | B then E | C then E |

Related Problems: 67, 55, 28, 27, 4

Problem Extension

Suppose hallway F is in the second building so the second building has three hallways. Now how many ways are there to walk from the entrance to the exit? (*9*)

STRATEGY ASSESSMENT IDEAS

Listen and watch as students work to see if they

- can give one way to get through the museum
- organize entries in the list
- list all possible entries

80 PROCESS PROBLEM

Before Kip left the museum, he stopped at the Museum Store to buy some souvenirs. He chose some rubber prehistoric animals and took them up to the counter. He bought 3 different animals and spent 12¢. Which animals did he buy?

Understanding the Problem

- What did Kip do before he left the museum? (*bought some rubber animals*)
- What is a souvenir?
- How many different kinds of animals are in the boxes? (*6*)
- How much does a rubber elephant cost? (*7¢*)
- What animal costs 5¢? (*turtle*)
- How many animals did Kip buy? (*3*)
- How much did he pay? (*12¢*)
- Did he buy more than one of the same kind of animal? (*no*)

Solving the Problem

- Could Kip have bought only an elephant and a turtle? (*no, he bought 3 animals*)
- Could Kip have bought a fish, a turtle, and a snake? (*no, he paid 12¢*)
- Can you guess which animals he bought and then add to check your guess? (*see solution*)

Solution

Guess and Check

- Try 7¢ + 2¢ + 1¢ = 10¢ (*too low*)
- Try 8¢ + 2¢ + 1¢ = 11¢ (*too low*)
- Try 8¢ + 3¢ + 1¢ = 12¢ (*correct*)
- Try 7¢ + 3¢ + 2¢ = 12¢ (*correct*)

Kip could have bought an elephant, a snake, and a fish; or a dinosaur, a bird, and a snake.

Related Problems: 68, 56, 40, 39, 16

Problem Extensions

1. Suppose Kip bought 3 different animals and only paid 10¢. What did he buy? (*fish, turtle, snake; or elephant, fish, bird*)
2. Suppose Kip bought 4 animals and paid 11¢. What did he buy? (*fish, turtle, bird, snake*)

STRATEGY ASSESSMENT IDEAS

Listen and watch as students work to see if they

- make guesses that indicate an understanding of problem
- use previous guesses to make better guesses
- check guesses using the information given in the problem
- give appropriate reasons for their guesses

ASSESSMENT APPENDIX

This appendix contains four tools to help you assess your students' progress.

Strategy Implementation Checklist

The Strategy Implementation Checklist contains characteristics of student performance related to each problem-solving strategy. These characteristics can be used to assess student progress over time in their ability to use strategies appropriately. Also, the specific performance characteristics can be used to analyze which aspects of implementing particular strategies students can carry out and which they cannot carry out.

Problem-Solving Observation Checklist

The *Problem-Solving Observation Checklist* includes general problem-solving behaviors and dispositions to be observed and analyzed over time. The first three items address students' selection and use of problem-solving strategies. Item 4 refers to the general approach students use to solve problems, and items 5 and 6 refer to students' dispositions related to solving problems. This checklist can be used as you observe students working in groups solving problems and as you analyze student work on a problem and reflect on their behavior and dispositions.

Focused Holistic Assessment Rubric

The five-level *Focused Holistic Assessment Rubric* is a holistic system for assessing written work, including students' written solutions to problems and, possibly, their written explanations of their problem-solving processes. This assessment method is a *holistic* method because it focuses on the total solution. It is a *focused* method because one number is assigned to a student's work according to specific criteria related to the thinking processes involved in solving problems. To use the rubric, begin by asking whether the student's paper meets any of the criteria listed under *4 Points*. If so, assign that paper 4 points. If not, move on to the *3 Points* category, and so on.

Mathematics Portfolio Profile Checklist

The intended purpose of a portfolio determines its contents and the method used to assess it. One common use of portfolios is as a collection of student work that can be analyzed for growth over time—that is, to give you a profile of the student's growth in mathematics. It is best to use a small number of criteria to develop such a profile. The following three criteria for the evaluation of portfolios are particularly appropriate for the primary grades:

- the ability to engage in problem solving and mathematical reasoning
- the use of oral, written, and visual modes—approaches or methods of doing mathematical activities—to describe mathematical concepts and relations
- the development of healthy dispositions toward mathematics

The *Mathematics Portfolio Profile Checklist* is designed with these three criteria in mind.

Strategy Implementation Checklist

Strategy	Criterion
MAKE A TABLE / LOOK FOR A PATTERN	PLACES ITEMS CORRECTLY IN THE TABLE
	USES A PATTERN TO CORRECTLY EXTEND THE TABLE
	INTERPRETS THE TABLE TO ARRIVE AT THE CORRECT ANSWER
LOOK FOR A PATTERN	DESCRIBES THE PATTERN FORMED BY INFORMATION IN THE PROBLEM
	EXTENDS THE PATTERN CORRECTLY
	USES THE PATTERN TO ARRIVE AT THE ANSWER
DRAW A PICTURE	DRAWS APPROPRIATE PICTURES TO REPRESENT INFORMATION IN THE PROBLEM
	USES PICTURES APPROPRIATELY
	GIVES APPROPRIATE REASONS FOR USING PICTURES
GUESS AND CHECK	MAKES GUESSES THAT INDICATE AN UNDERSTANDING OF THE PROBLEM
	USES PREVIOUS GUESSES TO MAKE BETTER GUESSES
	CHECKS GUESSES USING THE INFORMATION GIVEN IN THE PROBLEM
	GIVES APPROPRIATE REASONS FOR GUESSES
MAKE AN ORGANIZED LIST	CREATES CORRECT ENTRIES FOR A LIST
	ORGANIZES ENTRIES IN THE LIST
	LISTS ALL POSSIBLE ENTRIES
USE LOGICAL REASONING	USES A PLAN FOR RECORDING REASONING
	CORRECTLY USES ALL CONDITIONS GIVEN IN THE PROBLEM
	ARRIVES AT CORRECT CONCLUSIONS THROUGH REASONING

STUDENT

Problem-Solving Observation Checklist

STUDENT _____

DATE _____

	Frequently	**Sometimes**	**Never**
1. Selects appropriate solution strategies.	_____	_____	_____
2. Accurately implements solution strategies.	_____	_____	_____
3. Tries a different solution strategy when stuck (without help from the teacher).	_____	_____	_____
4. Approaches problems in a systematic manner (clarifies the question, identifies needed data, selects and implements a solution strategy, checks solution).	_____	_____	_____
5. Shows a willingness to try problems.	_____	_____	_____
6. Demonstrates self-confidence.	_____	_____	_____

STUDENT _____

DATE _____

	Frequently	**Sometimes**	**Never**
1. Selects appropriate solution strategies.	_____	_____	_____
2. Accurately implements solution strategies.	_____	_____	_____
3. Tries a different solution strategy when stuck (without help from the teacher).	_____	_____	_____
4. Approaches problems in a systematic manner (clarifies the question, identifies needed data, selects and implements a solution strategy, checks solution).	_____	_____	_____
5. Shows a willingness to try problems.	_____	_____	_____
6. Demonstrates self-confidence.	_____	_____	_____

© Addison-Wesley Publishing Company, Inc.

Focused Holistic Assessment Rubric

4 POINTS
These papers have any of the following characteristics:
- The student made an error in carrying out an appropriate solution strategy. However, the error does not reflect misunderstanding of the problem or lack of knowledge of how to implement the strategy, but is a copying or a computational error.
- The student selected and implemented appropriate strategies and gave the correct answer in terms of the data in the problem.

3 POINTS
These papers have any of the following characteristics:
- The student implemented a solution strategy that could have led to the correct solution but misunderstood part of the problem or ignored a condition in the problem.
- The student applied an appropriate solution strategy, but
  a. answered the problem incorrectly for no apparent reason,
  b. gave the correct numerical part of the answer but did not label it or labeled it incorrectly, or
  c. gave no answer
- The student gave the correct answer and apparently selected appropriate solution strategies, but the student's implementation of the strategies is not completely clear.

2 POINTS
These papers have any of the following characteristics:
- The student used an inappropriate strategy and obtained an incorrect answer but showed some understanding of the problem.
- The student applied an appropriate solution strategy, but
  a. did not carry it out far enough to find the solution (e.g., the student made the first 2 entries in an organized list), or
  b. implemented the strategy incorrectly, leading to no answer or to an incorrect answer
- The student successfully reached a subgoal, but could go no farther.
- The student gave the correct answer, but
  a. the work is not understandable, or
  b. no work is shown

1 POINT
These papers have any of the following characteristics:
- The student made a start toward finding the solution—beyond just copying data from the problem—that reflects some understanding of the problem, but the approach used would not have led to a correct solution.
- The student began with an inappropriate strategy and did not carry it out, with no evidence that the student turned to another strategy.
- The student apparently tried to reach a subgoal but never did.

0 POINTS
These papers have any of the following characteristics:
- The student left the paper blank.
- The student simply recopied the data in the problem, but either did nothing with the data or did something that appears to show no understanding of the problem.
- The student gave an incorrect answer and showed no other work.

Mathematics Portfolio Profile Checklist

STUDENT _____   **Substantial Growth**   **Some Growth**   **No Growth**

PROBLEM SOLVING AND REASONING

1. Understands information given in problems   _____   _____   _____
2. Applies strategies to solve problems   _____   _____   _____
3. Draws logical conclusions and gives reasons for them   _____   _____   _____

ORAL, WRITTEN, AND VISUAL MODES

1. Relates manipulatives, pictures, and diagrams to mathematical ideas and situations   _____   _____   _____
2. Relates everyday languages to mathematical language and symbols   _____   _____   _____

MATHEMATICAL DISPOSITION

1. Has confidence in ability to do mathematics   _____   _____   _____
2. Takes risks exploring mathematical ideas and trying alternatives   _____   _____   _____
3. Perseveres in mathematics activities   _____   _____   _____
4. Is interested in doing mathematics   _____   _____   _____

STUDENT _____   **Substantial Growth**   **Some Growth**   **No Growth**

PROBLEM SOLVING AND REASONING

1. Understands information given in problems   _____   _____   _____
2. Applies strategies to solve problems   _____   _____   _____
3. Draws logical conclusions and gives reasons for them   _____   _____   _____

ORAL, WRITTEN, AND VISUAL MODES

1. Relates manipulatives, pictures, and diagrams to mathematical ideas and situations   _____   _____   _____
2. Relates everyday languages to mathematical language and symbols   _____   _____   _____

MATHEMATICAL DISPOSITION

1. Has confidence in ability to do mathematics   _____   _____   _____
2. Takes risks exploring mathematical ideas and trying alternatives   _____   _____   _____
3. Perseveres in mathematics activities   _____   _____   _____
4. Is interested in doing mathematics   _____   _____   _____

© Addison-Wesley Publishing Company, Inc.

BLACKLINE MASTERS

GRADE 1

SECOND EDITION

PROBLEM-SOLVING EXPERIENCES IN MATHEMATICS

RANDALL I. CHARLES FRANK K. LESTER, JR. ANNE M. BLOOMER

Dale Seymour Publications®

Dale Seymour Publications
An imprint of Pearson Learning
299 Jefferson Road, P.O. Box 480
Parsippany, New Jersey 07054-0480

www.pearsonlearning.com
1-800-321-3106

Text Design: Betsy Bruneau Jones
Illustrations: Cynthia Swann Brodie, Joan Holub, Heather King

Copyright © 1996, 1985 by Addison-Wesley Publishing Company, Inc.

All rights reserved. Printed in the United States of America. This publication is protected by Copyright and permissions should be obtained from the publisher prior to any prohibited reproduction, storage in a retrieval system, or transmission in any form or by any means, electronic, mechanical, photocopying, recording, or likewise. The publisher hereby grants permission to reproduce these pages in part or whole, for classroom use only. For information regarding permission(s), write to Rights and Permissions Department. This edition is published simultaneously in Canada by Pearson Education Canada.

Dale Seymour Publications® is a registered trademark of Dale Seymour Publications, Inc.

ISBN 0-201-49361-6

4 5 6 7 8 9 - ML - 06 05 04 03 02 01

This Book Is Printed on Recycled Paper

1 Set 1
Grandpa's Train

© Addison-Wesley Publishing Company, Inc.

PROBLEM-SOLVING EXPERIENCES IN MATHEMATICS

1 LEVEL

3 Set 1
Grandpa's Train

© Addison-Wesley Publishing Company, Inc.

PROBLEM-SOLVING EXPERIENCES IN MATHEMATICS **1** LEVEL

4 Set 1
Grandpa's Train

© Addison-Wesley Publishing Company, Inc.

PROBLEM-SOLVING EXPERIENCES IN MATHEMATICS **1** LEVEL

1

2

3

4

5

Clues

1. I have a stem.

2. I have a smile.

3. I have 3 teeth.

Who am I?

8 Set 3
The Pet Store

© Addison-Wesley Publishing Company, Inc.

PROBLEM-SOLVING EXPERIENCES IN MATHEMATICS

LEVEL **1**

9 Set 3
The Pet Store

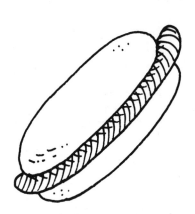  

7 tickets   5 tickets   6 tickets

3 tickets   3 tickets   4 tickets

BANANA STICKERS · 3¢ each

Number of Stickers	1	2	3	4	5
Cost	3¢	6¢	9¢		

16 Set 5 Sticking Together

HAPPY FACE STICKERS
2 stickers for 5¢

Number of Stickers	2	4	6	8	10
Cost	5¢	10¢	15¢		

18 Set 6
Getting Ready for Winter © Addison-Wesley Publishing Company, Inc.

PROBLEM-SOLVING EXPERIENCES IN MATHEMATICS — LEVEL 1

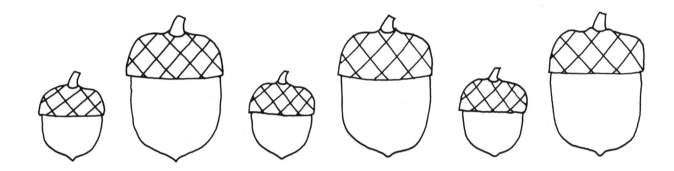

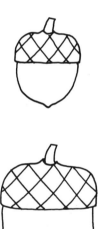

What comes next?

21 Set 7
The Circus

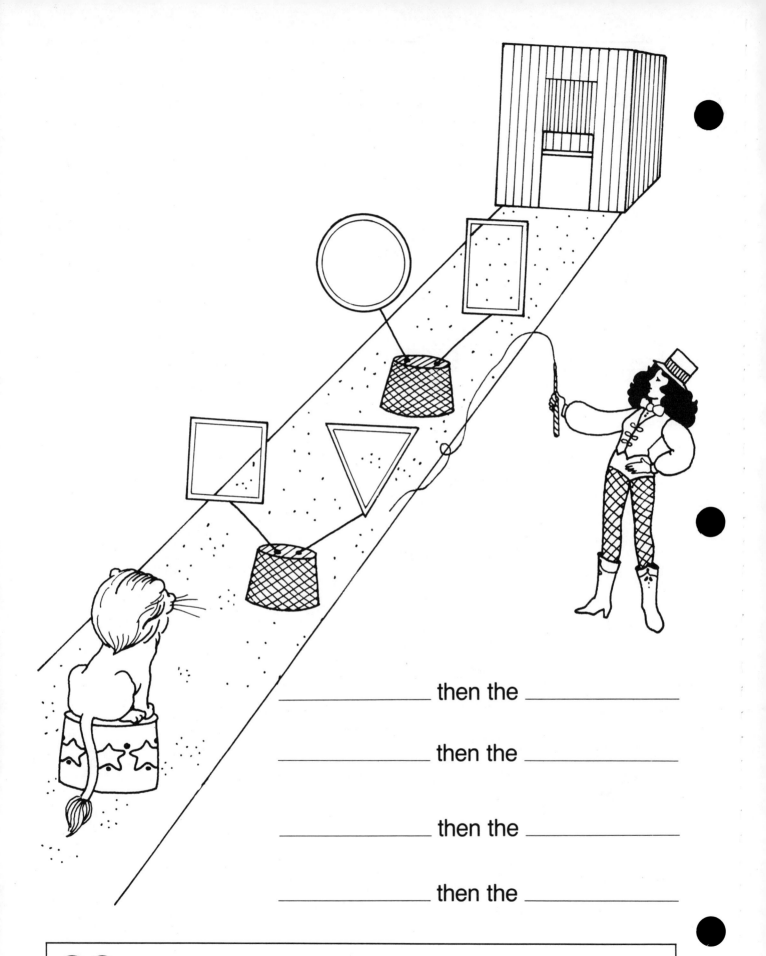

_____ then the _____

_____ then the _____

_____ then the _____

_____ then the _____

22 Set 7
The Circus © Addison-Wesley Publishing Company, Inc. PROBLEM-SOLVING EXPERIENCES IN MATHEMATICS LEVEL 1

_____ sneakers and _____ skirt

_____ sneakers and _____ skirt

_____ sneakers and _____ skirt

_____ sneakers and _____ skirt

_____ sneakers and _____ skirt

_____ sneakers and _____ skirt

Leo

Kate

Clara

Zeke

_____   _____   _____   _____

Winner

Zeke Zebra

Morris Monkey

Ellie Elephant

Clara Giraffe

Horace Hippo

26 Set 8
A Trip to the Zoo

© Addison-Wesley Publishing Company, Inc.

PROBLEM-SOLVING EXPERIENCES IN MATHEMATICS

LEVEL 1

27 Set 9
The Carrot Gardens

28 Set 9
The Carrot Gardens

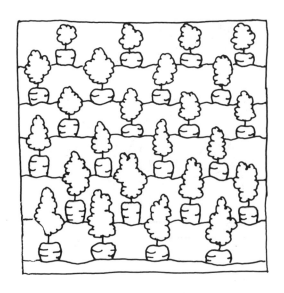
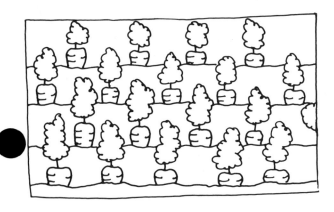

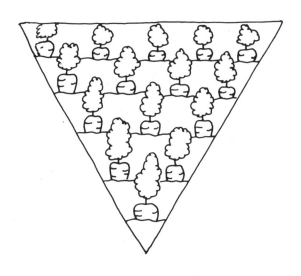

29 Set 9
The Carrot Gardens

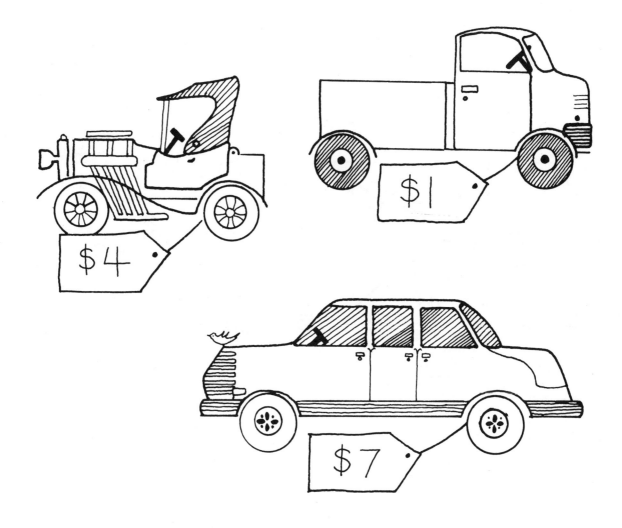
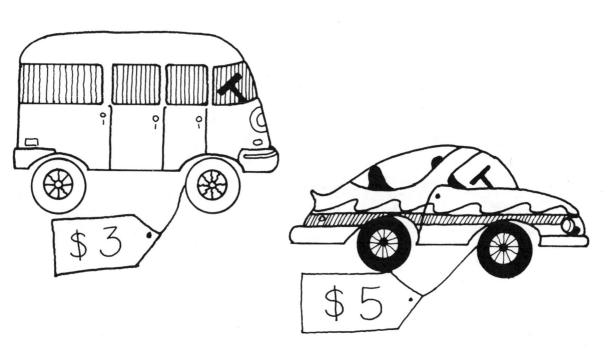

33 Set 10
Winnie's Toy Store

Number of Rides	1	2	3	4	5	6
Number of Tickets Needed	2	4	6	8		

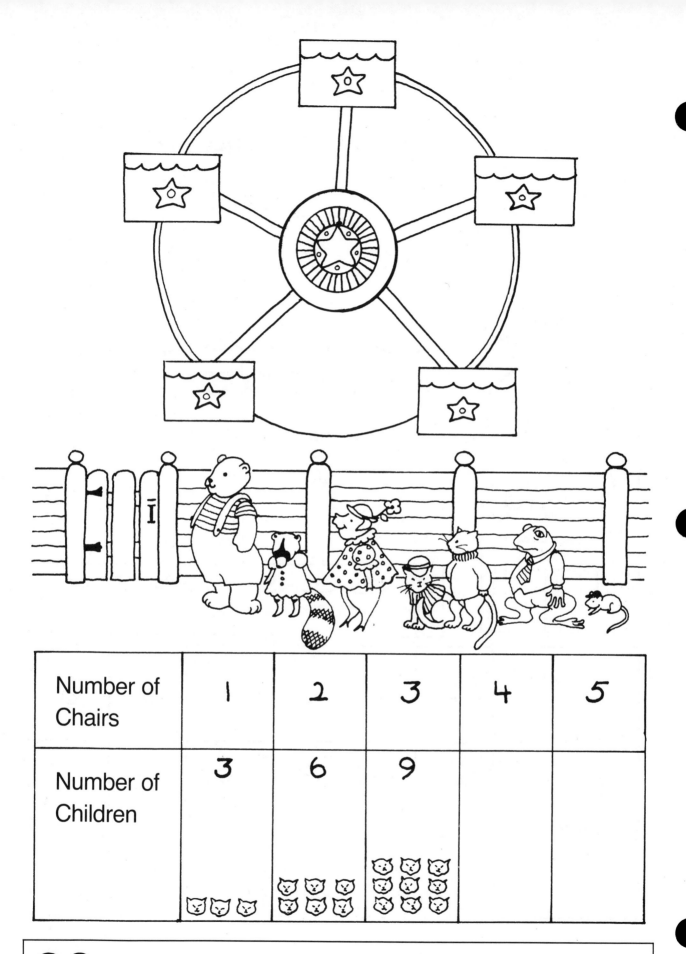

Which comes next?

Who comes next?

40 Set 13
At the Pond
© Addison-Wesley Publishing Company, Inc.

PROBLEM-SOLVING EXPERIENCES IN MATHEMATICS   LEVEL 1

41 Set 13
At the Pond

42 Set 13 At the Pond   © Addison-Wesley Publishing Company, Inc.   PROBLEM-SOLVING EXPERIENCES IN MATHEMATICS   **1** LEVEL

43 Set 13
At the Pond

45 Set 14
Pizza Party

© Addison-Wesley Publishing Company, Inc.

PROBLEM-SOLVING EXPERIENCES IN MATHEMATICS

1 LEVEL

Day	1	2	3	4	5
Number of Fish Caught	1	4	7		

48 Set 15
Penguins in the Snow   © Addison-Wesley Publishing Company, Inc.

PROBLEM-SOLVING EXPERIENCES IN MATHEMATICS   LEVEL 1

Day	1	2	3	4	5	6
Number of Snowballs Melted	1	2	4	7		

49 Set 15
Penguins in the Snow

PROBLEM-SOLVING EXPERIENCES IN MATHEMATICS

LEVEL 1

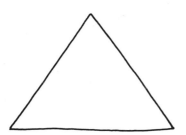

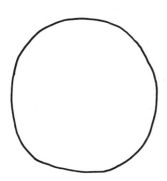

51 Set 16
Happy Valentine's Day   © Addison-Wesley Publishing Company, Inc.

PROBLEM-SOLVING
EXPERIENCES IN
MATHEMATICS   **1** LEVEL

52 Set 16
Happy Valentine's Day   © Addison-Wesley Publishing Company, Inc.

PROBLEM-SOLVING EXPERIENCES IN MATHEMATICS   **1** LEVEL

_____ shirt and the _____ shorts

_____ shirt and the _____ shorts

_____ shirt and the _____ shorts

_____ shirt and the _____ shorts

Number of Dog Yummies	1	2	3	4	5
Total Cost	3¢	5¢	7¢		

57 Set 18
More Pets

© Addison-Wesley Publishing Company, Inc.

PROBLEM-SOLVING EXPERIENCES IN MATHEMATICS

LEVEL 1

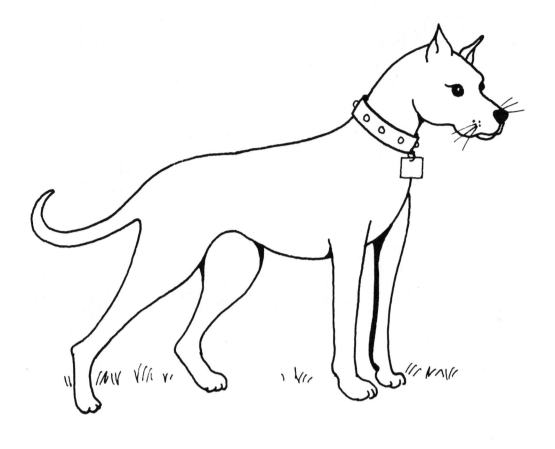
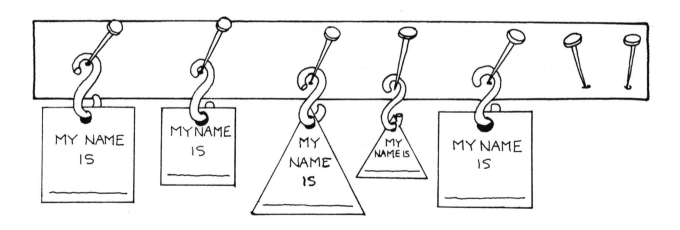

	Game 1	Game 2	Total
Bert	63	35	
Cindy	42	53	

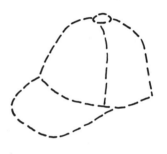

61 Set 19
Sports and Games

© Addison-Wesley Publishing Company, Inc.

PROBLEM-SOLVING EXPERIENCES IN MATHEMATICS

1 LEVEL

	Game 1	Game 2	Game 3	Game 4	Game 5
Rockets	2	4	6		
Cowboys	5	6	7		

MAP

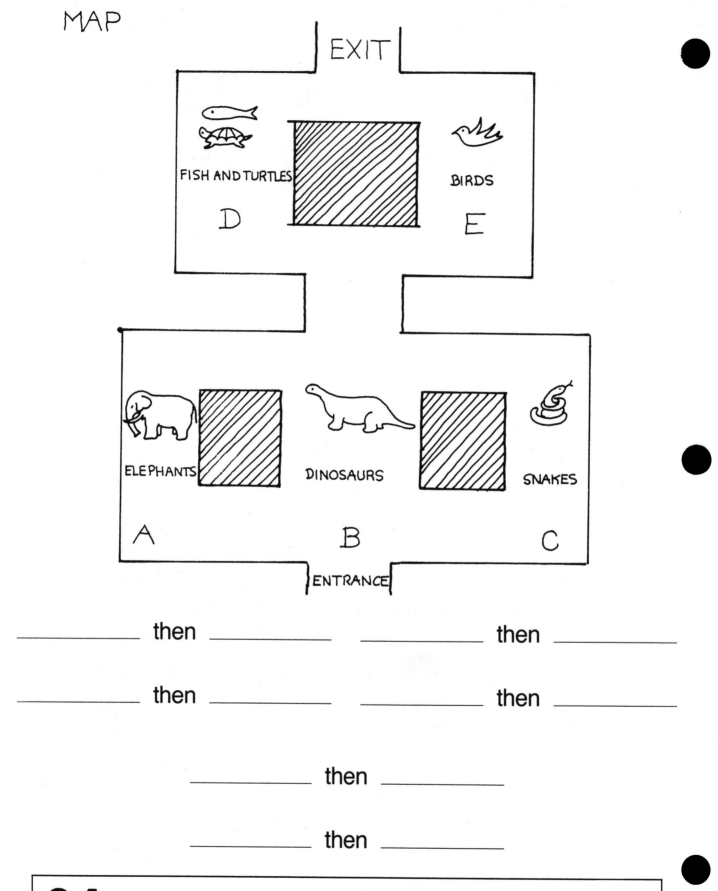

_____ then _____   _____ then _____

_____ then _____   _____ then _____

_____ then _____

_____ then _____

MUSEUM STORE

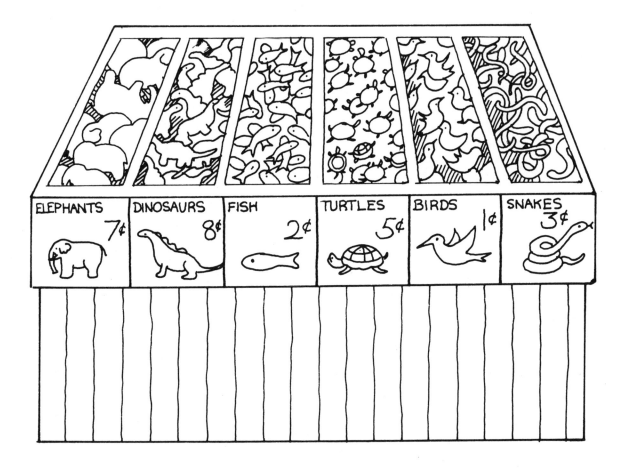

Problem-Solving Experiences in Mathematics—the highly successful program widely used in grades 1 through 8—has been expanded to include kindergarten! Along with the brand new kindergarten edition are revised editions of grades 1 and 2.

Teachers have praised *Problem-Solving Experiences in Mathematics* because it is easy to use, logical, consistent, and thorough. As students work independently, in cooperative groups, or as a whole class, they learn to approach mathematics problems systematically.

In the primary grades, *Problem-Solving Experiences in Mathematics* now incorporates the use of manipulatives into problem-solving strategies, such as make an organized list and look for a pattern. Assessment ideas, embedded in the activities and detailed in the Assessment Appendix, make it easier for teachers to incorporate formal assessment practices into established classroom procedures.

The 20 sets of lessons for grade 1 are grouped by story theme and include four types of problem-solving experiences:

- Problem-Solving Readiness Activities—to build confidence and prepare for real-world encounters

- Problem-Solving Skill Activities—to develop thinking processes

- One-Step Problems—to provide practice in translating story situations into number sentences

- Process Problems—to offer experience and guidance in the identification and use of the most common problem-solving strategies

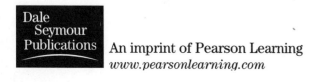

Dale Seymour Publications
An imprint of Pearson Learning
www.pearsonlearning.com

ISBN 0-201-49361-6